THE HUMANIST

A Short Life Sketch of Dr. Indira Goswami

by

AMAR KRISHNA PAUL

AKANSHA PUBLISHING HOUSE
NEW DELHI-110 059 (INDIA)

AKANSHA PUBLISHING HOUSE
R-37B, Vani Vihar, Uttam Nagar,
New Delhi-110 0059 (INDIA)
Phone : 5640621
Email : ektabooks@yahoo.com

The Humanist
First Published 2002

ISBN 81-87606-25-0

PRINTED IN INDIA

Published by M.P. Misra for Akansha Publishing House, New Delhi
and Printed at ARORA Offset Press, New Delhi.

This book is dedicated to
Late Radhika Mohan Mitra, my grandfather
For the uncompromising principles that guided his life;
Late Rai Mohan Paul, my grandfather
For leading his children into worthy pursuits; and
Late (Prof.) Shanti Ranjan Dey, my teacher
For making everything worthwhile.

— Author

Acknowledgment

Authoring a biographical book is not an easy task. But my self-confidence and firm determination, enriched by my spiritual *gurus*, teachers, friends and family members, helped my writing flow to grow and author a few books on biographies. To go ahead, I have completed, first of all, the book *The Humanist* (A biography of Mamoni Raisom Goswami or Dr. Indira Goswami).

I must thank Mr. Rajnath Pal and his wife Mrs. Indumati Rajnath for directly helping me to complete the book in time. I am greatly indebted to Mr. M. P. Misra, the publisher for bringing out the book. Dr. Hiren Gohain and Mrs. Rani Gohain encouraged me to grow in journalism all the time. I owe to them a lot. Others who helped me are — Manoj Jain, Kamal Krishna, Anamika Chakraborty, B. Paul, N. Paul, Ranjit Boro, B.B. Sen, (senior journalist), Rigved Sen, K.K. Purkayastha (G.M., G.L. Publications Ltd.), B.K. Nath, (Managing Editor, Economic Daily), N.N. Deka, B. Narzary, Dr. S.K. Das, Shankar Pal, Hemanta Deka, Golap Nath, Kameswar Boro, Prof G.G. Banik, Nilutpal Bhuyan, Anindya Gogoi, Chandan Sharma, Asim Baruah, Radhikamohan Bhagawati, Dr Parthsarathi Dutta, Anirban Roy, Monimoy Dasgutpta, Tapan Buzarbaruah, Chandrakanta Mahanta and so on. My writer-friends like Manbendra Bhattacharya, Abhijit Misra and Radha Verma — always exchanged views for improving the 'insight' of the work. I must thank all of them. All the teaching and non-techning staff of Kalibari Sishuniketan, Tangla Model High School and Tangla College helped me a lot. I am much obliged to them.

Above all, I am very grateful to my assistants D.D. Sarma and Miss Poly Buragohain for taking pain in D.T.P. works. Suggestion and constructive criticisms, which may be taken into consideration while preparing future edition of the book, are highly solicited.

January 6, 2002 **Amar Krishan Paul**
Guwahati (India).

Contents

1

Introduction

My books are my children, says Mamoni Raisom Goswami

Mamoni Raisom Goswami and President K.R. Narayanan addressed a cultural programme in New Delhi.

A relentless crusader for human values and social justice, Dr Indira Goswami alias Mamoni Raisom Goswami, is a celebrated name not only in Assamese literature but also in Hindi literature. In the book, *Masterpiece of Indian Literature*, Volume I, published by National Book Trust of India, she has been stated as the greatest woman writer in Assam today. The eminent writer has always been at ease with laurels that have had come her way. After the Sahitya, Katha and other awards, she was rightly conferred the 36th Jnanpith Award for the year 2000, the highest literary award in India.

The award carries a cash of Rs 5 lakh, besides a citation, plaque and a bronze replica of Vagdevi. Indira Goswami is the second Assamese writer to be honoured with the award. The selection board headed by renowned jurist and Rajya Sabha MP LM Singhvi chose Goswami for the award for 2000 at its meeting held on July 28, 2001.

> "Indira Goswami is one of the top Indian writers who have made a significant contribution to various branches of literature. Her canvas is wide and includus impressions of life and people in all their spectacular varieties and richness," the Jnanpith selection board stated.

Dr Goswami has been a strong contender for this national award for years, with her searing portraiture of human suffering, her commitment to truth at all costs and her profound compassion. It is a mark of the Jnanpith trust's concern for quality and excellence that she has been awarded the prize she so richly deserves. Every Assamese should feel proud that a compatriot has proved her high creative merit against rigorous standards. It is an indication of the growing maturity and depth of contemporary Assamese literature.

How does she want her progeny to remember her? In an AIR phone-in-conversation following the news of her being awarded the highest literary honour of the nation, she replied, "I shall feel well rewarded if the progeny reminisces me as a humanist."

Participating in an interactive programme between the author and the readers, Dr. Goswami implored not to categorise her just as a feminist as she rightly termed herself: *"I am a humanist"*.

Stating that in her writings she draws the pictures of the fate of humanity at various levels, she said, "It's true that authors cannot show the humanity a concrete route for a change, but they can definitely make them realise their own naked reality and situations."

Dr. Goswami has honoured the grand heritage of Assamese literature by becoming the second Assamese to be honoured with the 'Jnanpith' after Dr. Birendra Kumar Bhattachaya in 1979.

A bold narrator of human situations and social phenomena, Dr. Goswami carved a niche for herself at an early age. She authored over 25 novels and hundreds of short stories. She did several research works on the *Ramayana.* She enriched the Indian literary world through her translated works from Assamese to English, Hindi and also from other languages to Assamese.

All her outstanding creations are vitally based on realistic study of the existing social framework. The famous novel *Mamore Dhora Torowal* (1980) was written in the backdrop of labour strike in Uttar Pradesh and *Neelkanthi Braja* (1976), another socially acclaimed novel, reflected the lifestyle of the widows in Vrindavan. Her other notable novels are: *Tez Aru Dhulire Dusharita Pristha, Senabor Sront, Ahiron, Datal Hatir Unye Khowa Howda.* She has authored over one thousand short stories in Assamese too. Many of her writings have been translated in different Indian languages and English. Few of her works have been translated into Hindi e.g. *Ramayana: From Ganga to Brahmaputra,* a research-book.

Presently, she is a professor in the Department of Modern Indian Languages and Literary Studies, Delhi University. Earlier, she headed of this department dealing in 15 major Indian languages.

Her latest novel *Chinnamasta* on some naked facts around the Kamakhya shrine is now ready for publication. Portions of the novel published earlier by an Assamese magazine has provoked some quarters to the effect that she has reportedly received a few threats. The writer, known for her bold spirit, however maintains she would not budge an inch from her perceptions in the novel.

A humanist to the core, she is touched to see all kinds of afflictions suffered by humanity. But she believes, for most of his afflictions man is himself to blame and therefore he can only set things right.

As regards her personal profile, though Dr Goswami passed a happy childhood, she had a grief-ridden married life. She entered into wedlock with Madhavan Raisom Ayenger, who hailed from Karnataka, on October 22, 1965. But as luck would have it, her husband died in a sad mishap at Chandrabhaga in Kashmir Valley while on his way to supervise a bridge construction work in 1967. Her 'conjugal bliss' did last for just a little longer than one and a half years. Late Madhavan was a Civil Engineer and in-charge of the construction activities of a good number of bridges in Kashmir under Hindustan Construction Limited in the 60s.

Mrs Goswami with her husband Madhavan Raisom Ayenger posed for a snap in Kashmir Valley in the early part of 1966.

Writing, however, turned out to be an unavoidable preoccupation and passion for Mamoni Raisom Goswami after the sudden passing of her husband in the prime of his life. As time ticked away, the feeling of loneliness proved to be excruciatingly unbearable for her, as she herself recounts in her autobiography. This and many other vicissitudes of life catapulted her creative self to a higher plane which saw her making her mark as a writer with a difference.

To a question if she has any children, she quipped : "My books are my children."

It is important to note that Dr Goswami helps all, especially the students of the Northeast studying in Delhi, in different ways. In this manner she seems to mitigate her grievances and pacify her bruised feelings.

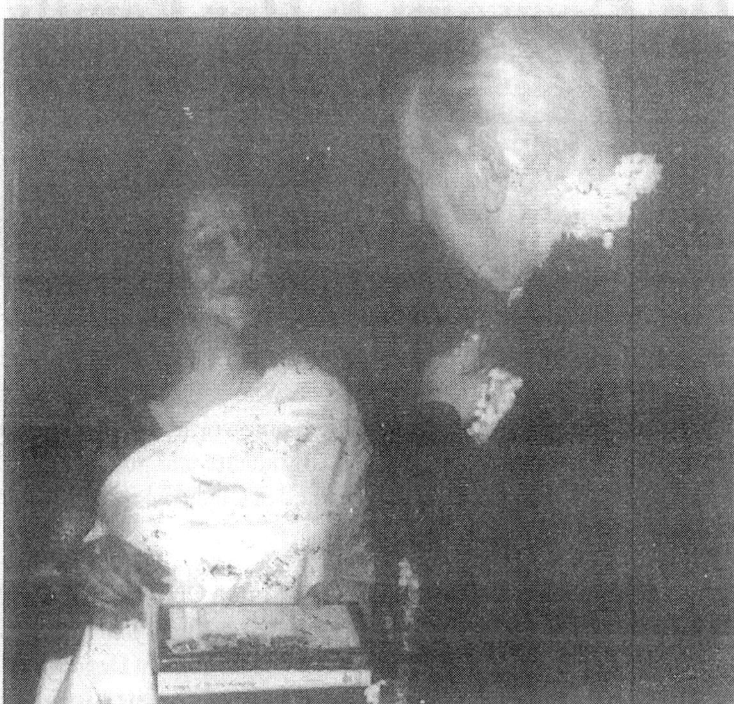

Dr. Indira Goswami with the Nobel Laureate, Simon Perez, former President of Israel.

2

Dr. Goswami & Her Family

Born on November 14, 1942 to an orthodox family at Guwahati (Assam), she passed a happy childhood. Her maiden name is Mamoni Goswami. The people's heart is filled with joy and pride when they say : "Our Mamoni !"

Dr Goswami got a rich family background. Late Uma Kanta Goswami is her father and Late Ambika Devi, her mother. Late Raghunath Goswami is her grandfather, who was the Sattradhikar (religious head) of Amranga Sattra. It is noteworthy that Late Uma Kanta Goswami, her father, was a postgraduate and gold medalist from Calcutta University. He had worked at Chand Morari College of Sylhet for a few days.

In 1933, he became the Principal of Cotton College, a premier academic institution in Northeast India. After three years he was inducted as a director-level bureaucrat in the Education Department of Undivided Assam under the British administration. He represented Assam before the Simon Commisssion for apprising the panel of the conditions and resources of the State economy at that time. He also worked diligently for the overall development of his native locality, Amranga Sattra. He and his brother, Chandrakanta Goswami together donated land and other property for the establishment of schools and hospitals.

In the words of Dr Goswami, "My father had an exceptionally brilliant academic career and won several gold medals, including a coronation memorial medal from the British Government in 1937.

He held several government posts, including the office of the Director of Public Instructions, of undivided Assam. At the same time, he carried out the duty of our Sattra. He appeared before the first Simon Commission and represented the Assam Government in the Economic Enquiry Committee held in Calcutta in 1925. Our forefathers originally came to Assam from Kanauj of Uttar Pradesh, and our Sattra or the religious monastery, peculiar to Assam, was founded 470 years ago by the Vaishnava Saint, Sri Santadeva disciple of Damodardeva who on the other hand was a disciple of the great saint Sankardeva.

Santadeva started preaching Vaishnavism on the south bank of the Brahmaputra, among the various hill tribes like Garo, Rabha and others. The kings of the small kingdoms, like the King of Rani, the King of Luki, and the King of Marupuria also became his disciples. King Shiva Singha who ruled in Assam in 1714 who donated vast areas of 'Nishpikheraj' (half taxable) lands to our Sattra, which was originally situated at a place called Garaimari. But Garaimari was destroyed in a devastating earthquake. The beautiful stone temple and other valuables of the Sattra were also damaged and destroyed. The Sattra was then transferred to a place called Jambori, then to Amranga, also situated on the south bank of the Brahmaputra. The vast areas of land enjoyed by my forefathers, were make 'Kheraj' (taxable) during the regime of General Jenkins."

She was very close to her father. In course of time, when Cancer stared him in his face she could feel her father staring at "the jaws of death".

She could not bear it. She thought of committing suicide. As she was unable to live without her father.

That is, death had cast its shadow over her since her childhood. But she was so ardently in love with her father that when she thought of his death which was inevitable in every individual's life she would feel so agitated that she should feel like drowning herself in the lake.

The newly-promulgated Land Acts under the new dispensation, at one stroke, deprived the landlords of their estates. But even then, on account of her father's status, coupled with her charms, she received offers of marriage almost everyday. But the fear that lay dormant in Indira's subconscious mind soon took its first toll. Her father met with an untimely death. As a result, offers of marriage from families with high profile which had become a daily ritual, suddenly stopped. Then a tendency of committing suicide had cropped up in her mind. It had degenerated into an obsession too. She began to think actively of it. She wanted to tread the path leading to the mysterious and unknown 'journey in space' from where no one ever returns.

In 1961, for many days she was found unconscious in the Civil Hospital at Guwahati. Then a time came when she had to face something much worse than the travails of the baptism of fire. It was the hell fire of society. People talked in whispers behind her back, "She must have conceived some serious matters. Imagine an unmarried girl becoming a mother ! That's why she took such a desperate step. That's why she wanted to commit suicide !!"

Then it suddenly dawned upon this pure virgin girl, this beautiful girl, what kind of world she would have to live in, if she had to live at all.

(L-R) Hridayananda Gogoi of Goriyosi, *Mrs Rani Gohain, Dr Goswami and author in Guwahati in 2001.* Picture by Kamal Krishna

3

Basics of Her Childhood

> *First of all, I would like to delve into the psychological mindset and principles of young people treading the path of violence and vengence : Dr Indira Goswami*

There is an interesting story of her childhood. When she was born, an astrologer had upset her parents by forecasting certain 'ominous' signs in her horoscope. The astrologer had a reason to worry. He had carefully studied and assessed what lay in store for this beautiful girl. According to his predictions, misfortunes would come upon her fast to bedevil her life. The astrologer had seen some peculiarity in Mamoni's horoscope what is not common in other's. And therein lay the whole snag. Whatsoever it is, he did not visualise the metamorphosis that the girl would undergo after her baptism of fire engendered by her misfortunes. Reading her future, the astrologer advised Uma Kanta and Ambika to leave behind 'the girl' afloat on the currents of the nearby river. Then her parents got worried. But they didn't follow the astrologer.

> If the same astrologer had been alive, he would have been ashamed of his prediction as Dr Goswami has reached the pinnacle of her pursuit in life till date by receiving many honours and awards in India and abroad.

At the present juncture she says: "I saw the deteriorating condition of this Sattra during my childhood. Most of the people became opium addicts. My father and others fought for de-addiction and rehabilitation of these opium eaters. My father also donated land in the Sattra for building a hospital. My forefathers used to keep numerous elephants. Sometimes elephants were sent to the forest for pulling out logs, and sometimes for catching wild elephants. Rani was the place in South Kamrup district of Assam where elephants were brought for training and domesticating. I went with my father many times to this countryside and watched the training of wild elephants in progress. The agony of the elephants being forced to carry out the commands of the trainer, left a deep impression on my mind, because I found it too cruel and a torture to a newly captured animal. My brother and I used to play with Rajendra, the last elephant left in the Sattra. Later on, this elephant ran amuck and killed a man. He had to be shot dead under a proclamation of the Government of Assam. Though a major part of my childhood was spent in Guwahati and Shillong still the days which I spent at our Sattra, left a lasting impression on my mind. I even wrote a voluminous novel on the background of this Sattra. Assam Sahitya Sabha has honoured me with their prestigious 'Basanti Devi Memorial award' for this novel."

Noted journalist Sanjay Hazarika addressed a meeting organised by Assam Association to felicitate Dr Goswami in Delhi in 2001.

4

Mixed Memories from Student Life

During school days, I thought I would be a writer. My experience of life was yet limited and vague; still I started writing, and tried to render sensitively in words my perceptions of life, however, inadequate : Dr Goswami.

She received her formal education at Latashil Primary School in Guwahati from 1947 to 1950. Thereafter, she and her sister, Sabita, left for Shillong. They got admission there at Pine Mount European School and studied up to 8th standard from 1950 to 1955. Latter on, she and her family returned to Guwahati and settled here in 1955.

"I did not want to leave Pine Mount European School. It was an English medium school. I had a cordial relations with the teachers there. Enchanting hills and natural scenic beauty of the 'Scotland of the East' won my heart. I was mighty charmed by the scenic sights of Shillong," she said recalling her sweet memories that attached with Pine Mount School.

There was no scope for learning Assamese at Pine Mount European School. But her parents took special care in teaching Assamese at home. Her father also instructed the private tuitor, who used to teach all subjects, to teach Assamese. Thus, her learning of the Assamese language actually began at home.

She said, "In fact, our farsighted father contended that we should read in Assamese medium school. We used to regard our benevolent father very much. We didn't dare to comment on his decision and will."

She came close in touch with a number of brilliant and affectionate teachers at T. C. High School. They never took fine for her absence as they were kind hearted.

In the words of Dr Goswami her teachers of Pine Mount School, Shillong were also benevolent. Some of the mistresses of Pine Mount School were Miss Holtin, Miss Neel, Miss North, Miss Souber and so on.

"Today, when I recall them, I do realise vividly how the teachers in those could draw lasting admiration from the students! At this juncture, I should also recall my revered teachers of T. C. High School. They were Mrs Indira Devi, Late Nilima Das, Mrs Anusoya Hajarika, Late Girija Das, Mrs Kalyani Phukan, Late Shakuntala Roychoudhury, Mrs Namita Das, Mrs Bhanumati Bora, Mrs Hiranmoyee Devi, Mrs Tamal Kusum Das, Late Doly Talukdar, Late Mandira Das, Mrs Roma Sarmah and so on. Mr Madan Deka was the lone male teacher in our school at that time. He taught us Mathematics and Science. Every teacher of T. C. Girls' High School used to keep vigil on all students so that they came to school wearing proper dresses. I was the Secretary of T. C. Girls' High School Union. At that time, freedom movement reached its acme. I used to ring the bell of our school, inviting the schoolstudents of Guwahati to join in the movement. We were members of Girls' Guides. Our teacher was Mr Rameswar Kalita. Sometimes he used to take us out for tracking. I still remember the visit to the camp at North Guwahati. Noted educationists Late Hiranaya Kumar Bhuyan and Late Dandeswar Gogoi also visited the camp with us. The lessons, that I learnt as a Scouts and Guide, inspired me to be self-reliant, hard-working and a disciplinarian. Myself, Gita Dutta and Padumi Kalita were selected for participating in the Jambori camp at Jaipur. Rameswar Kalita sir guided us. We had also to stage a rally there. I met an old man at Jaipur during that time. He accepted me as his daughter and wrote many letters to me. Those letters were kept with much care by my mother. He wrote about tragic incidents. In course of time I narrated his travails in one of my novels," Dr Goswami remarks.

Recalling her cherished memories in Shillong during school days she says : "I remember a British lady, Miss Holtin. She taught us swimming. She was jovial by nature and her face was always wreathed in smiles. It was her duty every Friday to take the Pine Mount girls to a club near Crinoline Falls for practice."

She had no swimming suit of her own. But she knew a girl of her age. That girl was the daughter of a Bengali cook who used to live in one of the outhouses of Mamoni. That girl and Mamoni used to play together.

"A girl who lived in the bungalow before we moved in, had given her that suit. It was, however, an old-fashioned piece. Since she was the daughter of a mere cook, she was not entitled to the privilege of studying in an exclusive school like the Pine Mount, meant only for the well-to-do. So, the suit was of no use to her. I took it from her, and wore it in Miss Holtin's practice classes. That was the time when father lavished his love and care upon me. But, somehow, I could not ask him for a swimming suit," she mutters.

Even today, she cannot guess what stood in the way. Her father was a frugal housekeeper. To keep all the family members warm from the severe cold of Shillong, he got two overcoats of his own choice tailor-made for Mamoni and her young sister. But her friends did not think much of her overcoat. Theirs were made with fine lining, but hers was of course yarn. But simply because it was her father's choice, she always attached a sentimental value to it and always kept it trim. Her schoolmates in Pine Mount were mostly from the upper sections of society. Naturally, their clothes were of the latest style.

Among her schoolmates, there were a few European girls. The happy memory of some of them still abides with her. There was Leslie Warner, mushroom-complexioned her hair like bees-wax. She was a blonde. And Ebon Neil, extremely fine and charming. Also, there was Florence Sails, stocky in build, and pockmarked. And many more besides. How they seem to float before her meditative eye !

Almost all of them celebrated their birthdays to which she was invited. Of her own birthday, she had, however, little idea, nor did the members of the family seem to remember it. Not just me, none of the children of the family celebrated his or her birthday. To observe a birthday did not, somehow, seem to be the practice. Her father was particularly keen to see that the children lived a simple life, free from ostentation and artificialities.

> "My father always insisted on plain living and high thinking as a matter of principle. Consequently, whenever I attended the birthday of some daughter of the high-ups, I sat in a corner, quiet as a dove. I had no raincoat either. And so, sometimes in the rain, I slipped out of the file when the Pine Mount girls were taken out for a picture," she brings in mind with pride.

She continued to attend Miss Holtin's swimming classes in that old, discarded suit. Yet she did not grieve, or complain, or grumble. At that time, she took lessons in tailoring from a Sicilian instructress, Miss Dwyrup. She was strong and stout, and had red, cropped hair, and upraised teeth. Her complexion war fair but her face was smudgy, so that she was far from beautiful in appearance. But at heart, she was extremely kind and affectionate.

In 1985, on her way to Florence and Pisa, Mamoni had been very close to Naples Capri and Ana Capri. She had a great desire to go to Sicily. But she did not know Miss Dwyrup's exact address, notwithstanding she had a strong desire to stand in front of her at her own door in Sicily. Miss Dwyrup, as she remembers, often spoke of Ana Capri and Florence. Even without seeing Miss Dwyrup for all these years and without being sure that she was still alive, Mamoni sought her in Ana Capri, frantically scanning, as it were, the shops and the churches of the town in the hope of meeting that dear old lady who meant so much to her as a young girl. The desperation and suicidal tendencies of the Shillong days seemed to have secured a foothold in her heart.

Even as a child, Mamoni was stricken with grief to think of the terrible effect of separation from her near and dear ones. She did not know what exactly it was. It was a sort of strange unease of her inner mind which she tried to subdue but failed.

> The Crinoline Falls, the lush green meadows of Lady Hydari Park and pine rows on the hills facing her bunglow in Shillong seemed to constitute the essence of her life.

Mamoni experienced peculiar sensations and feelings. Sometimes, she would wake up suddenly from sleep at midnight, and hear the shivering of the wind-tossed pine leaves. It sounded like the wailing of women in distress. She seemed to have often heard this plaintive cry. The pear trees beneath the slopes or on the edge of the house compound seemed to shine with their own distinct life and identity. Everything of the days in Shillong is evergreen in her mind - like images of flesh and blood, very much like the images of those kindly souls of old - Miss Dwyrup and Miss Holtin and many other familiar figures.

Miss Neil was the headmistress. She was a lady of multifaceted personality. Most of the time, Mamoni saw her busy with her office-work. Only when some girls committed a serious offence, she would have visited that class. On such occasions, she would carry a ruler with her. She used to ask the offending girl to extend her palm and then hit her with the ruler so mercilessly that every time Mamoni saw that brutal operation, she felt parched to the bone. Then her heart went out to the poor girl, and her eyes would brim with tears. A stout girl with the surname Golab Rai, often faced this ignominy. She is still vivid in Mamoni's memory.

Mamoni met Mrs. Rogers, the new headmistress of Pine Mound School, for a few days. She was a stout, plain looking lady, who always wore short frocks. She used to send lavish presents for my brothers and sisters.

> Mamoni's father was a man of integrity and high principles. Being the Director of Public Instruction, he did not like those gifts being given to his children.

After some years, she heard at Guwahati that Mrs. Rogers had obtained the posting with fake certificates and documents. When it came to light, she committed suicide out of remorse.

Another hearty figure, Mrs. Coleman, well-known for her roses, who used to teach drawing. For Mamoni, drawing was a craze. She once drew the picture of Jesus with a long beard. Mrs. Coleman showed it to other teacher who had gathered on the long porch of the school. In those days, Mamoni was a pupil of the first standard and could hardly express anything in English.

Once Mamoni had to be greatly excited as she was awarded certificate of merit in a drawing competition organised by Mrs. Coleman. The mouldy roll of this drawing perhaps lies crumpled somewhere with her old belongings. The picture of Jesus, Son of God, seemed to have been firmly set in her heart.

There is a church at the Police Bazar area of Shillong. From the verandah, Mamoni could be all ears for the tolling of the bells. She also visited once a fair organised by the church during days of holy X-Mas festival. She saw there some English men and women selling bouquets of flowers made of wollen cloth. A gaily decorated picture of Jesus was displayed in the fair.

What had first drawn her attention to it was the blotches caused by the hammering of nails into His body. The crown of thorns, too, pricked her heart. In those days, she covered all her exercise books with pictures of Jesus. She also attended at school the scripture lessons, although they were not compulsory for non-Christian girls.

In fact, very few non-Christians attended those lessons. These classes started with recitations in praise of Jesus. They were printed in booklets which were distributed among the pupils.

In her own words : "The compassion of Lord Jesus on the cross radiated itself through that mysterious halo that seems to be without a parallel. Occasions like those revived in me the memory of the familiar face of Jesus of my schooldays. Again, at the Vatican, the unexampled expression of pity which shone from the face of Jesus lying on the gap of Virgin Mary by Michelangelo transported me into a world of peace and bliss beyond words. Michelangelo was only twenty-five when he made this immortal sculpture, 'Piets'. My eyes grew misty out of a sense of deep gratitude as I pored over it. That day in the Vatican, I wiped my tears unseen. Gone are the days when I had sketched Jesus with a long beard. It's long since I abandoned my brush and paint and easel. Yet, even today I feel moved to the depths of my being when I see a picture of Jesus on the Cross. It was Mrs. Coleman who encouraged me to draw and paint when I was a mere child. Where has she now gone? Shall I see her again? Gone forever like Mrs. Powell who taught us English songs, like Miss Seith who encouraged us to write essays! Gone are they all : Miss Dwyrup, Miss Neil, Miss Holtin, Miss Sweney, Mrs, James! They came in my life, as it were, to initiate me into the terrible affliction of separation from loved ones. Only their indelible prints upon my mind endure. So, it happens in life, it always does. Towards the end of my stay at Shillong, I had encountered some strange experiences. Those were the experiences of a girl slowly growing up to womanhood. I grew aware of my figure filling out day by day. I would have, If I could hidden my norm from others view. At the age of twelve, my breasts had grown so that I was terribly embarrassed, when my father saw me, taking a bath naked in the bathroom. Again one day, as I was coming out from the swimming pool, I saw a Christian youth goggling ravenously at my figure. I went to see films of all sorts."

It is worthwhile to note that 'Samson and Delilah' was the one that Mamoni went to see over and over again. Then she felt much excited to see the American cine-star, Victor Mature, playing Samson. It was a passion of sorts which only she could not define.

Describing her cherished memories she says : "I remember how I entreated the visitors to the family to take me with them to see 'Samson and Delilah' at the Garrison cinema. Many of them were amused at my request. Others promised they would, but not a single one of them cared to take me along. I longed to go and see Victor Mature in person."

> It follows from above that she got admitted at Tarini Choudhury Girls' High School adjacent to Guwahati Club area. After passing school final examination, she appeared for intermediate exam in 1959 from Handique Girls' College, Guwahati. She came out with flying colours. She passed B.A. with honours in Assamese and a special paper in Bengali from Cotton College in 1962. She obtained M.A. degree in Assamese from Gauhati University in 1964. Thus she pursued the greater part of her studies in Guwahati.

She said, "I tried my utmost to do well in the examinations but by and by I grew disillusioned about the methods of examinations as they then prevailed in our country. I had a brief stint as a teacher in a missionary school. I was drawn to the statue of Jesus on the cross seated at a corner of the school compound."

After receiving the Jnanpith Award, Mamoni Raisom Goswami was felicitated by JNU students and professors in Delhi in 2001.

5

Marriage and Afterwards

> *There was no dearth of lovers. They belonged to all classes - Hindus and Muslims, Brahmins and Kayasthas. But there was absolutely no question of physical love : Dr Goswami*

Yes, it was nothing but a sort of "love at first sight". She and her husband had fallen in love at the first sight before they got married. But it culminated in a short-lived marriage. For they lived together for one and half years only. As her husband expired in an accident, she had to pass difficult days and a 'tragedy'. She still recollects the 'sweet memories and tragedy' with her husband.

> It was the month of April, 1962. She met Karnataka's Mysore-based civil engineer Madhaben Raisom Ayenger (or Madhu). He worked for Hindustan Construction Company. He came with many other company officials to Guwahati for the construction of Saraighat Dalang, the first bridge over the river Brahmaputra.

As is well-known, she came with extraordinary wisdom and wit that would have been used for creative contribution to this world. Then how could she commit suicide? She turned out as spate of storied all of which had the distinction of being published. It was really something to gloat over. But her mother's mind was elsewhere. She was, however, worried about Mamoni's marriage. Nature dropped her a dear little hint."

Having said that a young engineer from Karnataka came to stay in her neighbourhood. After many days, many months, he made bold to talk to her. He was silently in love with her. The sunset over the Brahamaputra is a glorious sight. According to Mamoni, it was something divine. The young South Indian engineer was eager to enjoy this sight in her company. After an appropriate lapse of time the young engineer approached the mother for her daughter's hand in marriage. Indira's mother wanted to have an Assamese young man as a husband for her daughter and not a South Indian.

This introduced a note of discord in the young girl's life which began to look desolate and bleak to her. To counteract these effects the pundits suggested to her mother that she should perform Bagla Devi's puja. Bagla Devi was said to be another manifestation of Kali Devi.

It was said that Goddess demanded the sacrifice of a big black goat to appease her and blood should be applied as a bloodmark on her forehead. It was again an hour of ordeal for her.

While sitting in the temple for worship a shudder ran through her body at the very thought of goat's blood and she started crying. When the hot blood was smeared on her forehead as a sacred bloodmark, for many days thereafter it kept burning a hole in the forehead.

She tells the full story alike:

"Madhavan was busy at his work the whole day. In the evening, returning from the work-site, he would recline on an armchair, with a book in hand. I met him several times face to face as he was reading a book or driving his jeep to the site.

One day, I accompanied my brothers and sisters and the members of the family from whom Madhavan hired the house, for a picnic at a place near Sonapur. As could be expected, Madhavan, too, was with us. We settled on a spot on the bank of the river Umium where there was sort of improvised shelter of rectangular shape. From under that shelter, the river looked simply marvellous. There were dense forests on both sides of the river. The shadows reflected on the waters gave the impression of unfathomable depth. The waters of the river seemed to resemble those at that deep point of the Crinolin Falls which had aroused my curiosity in my childhood. As I was engrossed in watching the spectacle of glory of that the river, I was startled to find Madhavan Raisom slowly emerging into view and walking along the bank towards me. As I rose to greet him, he said, rather abruptly, 'For some time now I've been thinking of meeting you in such surroundings and alone.' 'Oh, really!' Straight out he said : 'Everyone should have an aim in life. What's yours, if you don't mind telling me?' I had no ready answer. Actually, I had no answer at all to that question. I only knew how to dig the graveyard in my thought. Then, in a voice filled with emotion, he said ; 'You're so lovely! But you hardly show it!' I still do not know what he saw worth admiring in my person."

Then, she continued to think that like many other well-wishers, Madhu, too, only tried to cheer her up. He must have heard that she had attempted suicide and had to be hospitalised.

From that meeting, she could know that she was closely observed by Madhu. Three years rolled by. All that long while, she was alive as it were, to the secession of the sacrificial blood on her forehead. As for her mother, failing to find a suitable match of her choice, she became very desperate.

In those days, she was a postgraduate student at that time.

Mamoni penned a number of short stories as she loved writing about her lost horizon. In the literary works, her sympathy went on to highlight those who were denied justice and were victims of oppression.

Sad to say, not even a single story came up to standard, according to her statement.

But she was indifferent to praise or adverse criticism. The hours devoted to literature gave her peace of mind. At other hours, her mind was lost in agony and strife.

It was the month of April in 1963. Madhu proposed to her.

He said, "I want to take you out of this place. You'll get a chance to move with me from one work-site to another work-site and record the life of the labourers. You'll see them from close quarters."

At that moment, she raised her eyes and looked at him around his face.

He further quipped : "I have been waiting for you for the last three years. I know your family will frown upon the very idea of your proposal to marry me, because I belong to the South. Yet, I am ready to talk to your mother."

Latter on, Madhu sounded her mother on the question but she dismissed him with cold contempt for his boldness.

Another year passed. Marriage for her still remained an elusive prospect. In desperation, her mother started looking for a match even in such families of which she could not at all approve. She nearly lost all restraint.

There was no dearth of lovers. They belonged to all classes - Hindus and Muslims, Brahmins and Kayasthas. But there was absolutely no question of physical love. Queer fellows, some of them were! Some wrote verses, some wrote her long letters praising her for the beauty of her body and mind. A few seemed satisfied by merely sauntering along the road in front of their house.

"There was one mad fellow who thought he loved me. He should be found lying, without any clothes on, at our gate and would appeal to every passerby in these words : 'This Gosain's daughter has thrust a thorn into my foot. Won't you ask her to draw it out? I was scared at the prospect of encountering him on the way. Even in the examination hall at Cotton College, I felt perplexed for fear that the lunatic might rush in and create a scene in the presence of all my teachers! I did not know the man's antecedents or the cause of his derangement. Ultimately, the fellow was handed over to the police. The scene is still vivid in my mind," she said.

Thus stories of those who professed their love for her are still fresh in her memory. Certainly they are providing enough material for a lively work of fiction.

Her mother's endless quest for finding her a match drove her frantic. One day, seized by an impulse to quit home, she stole out all by herself. A lover of mine had been waiting for her at a street corner. Once, he gave her a lift in his car to his place. She signed there, in the presence of a lawyer, certain marriage deeds which had been kept ready. Thus she was hastily made to go through a civil marriage ceremony after which she returned home with the assurance to return to him as soon as possible. Not for long, however, had she known this young man. He belonged to a caste different from Mamoni's.

That groom belonged to an Ahom family. Ahom people are originally from the Shan tribe of Upper Burma region, the tribe which came to Assam eight hundred years ago. Ahoms ruled Assam for six hundred years.

He was handsome in appearance, had been abroad for studies, and had an excellent job as the Director of Inland Water Transport of Assam then. Still, it seemed to her that he was lacking in something. She was not sure what that something was. But she knew, as if from instinct, that he lacked something.

How is it that she could not surrender herself to this man? She had put her seal of agreement on the marriage deeds, and yet had no mind to submit herself to him as his wife! It was a strange situation for her. She was in a fix. None of her family had any inkling yet about the development. A sense of shame and repentance and anguish made her miserable.

How could she be so heartless? How could she so sever her well-wishers? What a mean trick to play! Even a hardened sinner would think twice before doing such a turn to his own mother who was like a Goddess!

She began to feel brokenhearted. What was this love on her part?

How is it that she the least sympathy for the man who had been accepted by her as husband? For a moment, a strange thought came her, so she said to herself, but what would happen to Madhu who had offered to marry her? Out of all her lovers, for the first time in her life, she even started imagining a kind of physical bond with him.

> In those days, her mind was no less perplexed than when she had attempted suicide.

She grew restless. She would suddenly wake up in the middle of the night all bathed in sweat. She did not know what to do. She knew the man was anxiously waiting for her in his house on the bank of the Brahmaputra. With all the love in his heart he had accepted her as his wife. How then that she had kept him waiting without the slightest compunction? Why had she not been able to go to him? What was there to debar her? At that still hour of the night when everyone of the family was fast asleep, she could quietly slip out, unnoticed. She had already put her signature on the official deeds. Why, then, this trepidation? This hesitation?

The young man, her 'husband', was vexed that she did not join him. A natural reaction, of course. But she seemed to have no end of excuses. Then her younger brother was ill. The younger sister had her examination and that surely, was not the time to break her calm. Other thoughts also assailed her. What would happen to her sisters after her affair became public? What chance of marriage would they then have? How would mother then face the problem? These pertinent questions were repeatedly knocking her in those hard days.

So, she puts, "Inter-caste marriage is still a taboo in our society. In a society like ours, sectarian considerations get the better of human questions. What would my mother do? How would she help herself? She would get a fit if she knew what I had done!"

After the unfortunate demise of her father, they grew up under the protective care of their mother. The mother had been the only refuge in their moments of anxiety and grief. Without her, their life seemed to be without moorings. Yet, she had kept her in the dark about what she had done!

"I could not sleep at night. Nor could I find any way out of the impasse into which I had pushed myself. One night, I walked out and went even to the point of the farthest street light, and then suddenly recoiled. Hastily, I retreated. How was is that I could not go to him? To the man to whom I had pledged my loyalty as a wife? The door, I knew, was open," she narrates.

One day, Madhu met her on the way. In a voice choked with grief and pain, he said : "Our marriage has been contracted. Yet you've kept it a secret from your family, I know, I shall not wait any longer, be sure, unless you come of your own, I shall drag you to my place within a day or two."

Thus the affair of her civil marriage could no longer be hushed up. It could spread like wildfire. To recount the reaction in the family would make very unpleasant reading.

It was not in her power either to express it in all its details. Once again she appeared before a magistrate in the court at Mangaldoi where a number of well-wishers accompanied her. She signed on the dotted line. She had no idea even on that very day as to the kind of agreement she signed under Section 11 of the Civil Marriage Act. She was so depressed that she did not even glance at the papers. The heap of papers laid before her like a bundle of dry bones. After coming back home at Guwahati, she plunged for days into a well of dark depression. Again those sinister thoughts of self-annihilation haunted her mind!

For now she feels as if she was transformed into an automaton at that destined hour of her life. She could hardly raise her head to read the documents. The agony and shame of the entire episode made her insensate, as it were. Out of the court, she stepped into another world. In October 1965, along with other members of the family she went to their ancestral 'Sattra' (a Vaishnavite establishment) on the bank of the small river, Jagolia, which was her favourite place. There, in the same month, she was married to Madhavan Raisom Iyenger, according to Vedic rites. Like her, Madhavan also was a Brahmin. There would, therefore, be no material objection to her marrying him. After all, that had happened to her, mother hardly had the face to seek a match for her from the very own Assamese society.

After all that storm and stress, there came a day when she landed at Kunvarbet in the sandy tracts of the Rann of Kutch of Gujarat in the company of Madhavan, her husband.

The water of the mighty Arabian sea washed the shores and raised huge salt dumps. The entire area was a desert waste. She saw men and women from the nearby desert village of Khavda carrying away sackfuls of salt. The salt dumps shone in the sun like grains of silver. Madhavan was well-known for his technical expertise of the superstructure of a bridge. It is in connection with the building of a bridge that he went to Kutch. The bridge was to be mainly for the use of the army guarding the frontier, not for the use of the civilians. Its structural design was extraordinary. Special demolition chambers were built into it so that it could be blown up if a threat of an enemy attack materialised. Keeping that in view, certain hollow spaces of twenty feet height and five feet width were provided inside pillars of the size of fifty feet height and thirty feet width.

She used to visit the work sites with Madhu too.

For the first time in her life, she felt released from those nightmarish thoughts that had preyed upon her mind and spirit for long years of her childhood and youth.

She felt in her pulse, the freedom of the open blue sky over her head. Each new day was now a glory, a revelation. The desert strip of Kanvarbey lost its barrenness, as it were. The old desperation that had gnawed into her vitals was gone. The constant death wish that had oppressed her mind and body, was then a thing of the past. It was inconceivable for her to harbour any such thought, for how could that man do without her? The realisation slowly dawned upon her that the justification of their life laid not in itself, but in their earnest endeavour to live for others.

> One thing about Madhu came to her notice that he was deeply religious. He often carried with him a handy copy of the *Gita* wherever he travelled.

At the project site, they lived in thatched sheds. The labourers also lived in the same place. Madhu had at that time to shoulder very heavy responsibilities upon him; still, he could make it convenient to come and see her at intervals lest she felt forlorn or felt neglected in an alien land, far away from her home and her people.

Madhu used to take her to a village named Khavda to show her the unique splendour of the sun setting over the desert. The village was known for its large number of camels and the thorny shrubs and bushes. It was the village where she had enjoyed for the first time the rare spectacle of sunset over the desert. The rows of camels in the distance grew dim in the approaching darkness. Like ships afloat on the sea at sunrise, were the rows of camels. The last rays of the sun were scattered over a number of old, dilapidated forts situated on tracts of sand, looking like grains of bone. The sight was superb, beyond words. The sunbeams were to me like lean skeletons of golden-haired princesses flung in the plains. A cluster of only bare bones, without any trace of flesh.

There were also the thorny shrubs with tiny green leaves on which the camels browsed quietly. They seemed to lend to the evening setting of hallow hue, a sort of serenity and grace.

Going out to that sleepy village to enjoy the glory of sundown became a part of their daily routine. Much has she travelled in this wide world, but nowhere else has she seen as ruddy a sky.

The sun would flood, as it were, the whole arid expanse with its own radiance. The eerie beauty that the earth and the sky conspired to produced is indeed beyond words.

Madhu took her with him to many other places of uncommon attractions. They went to Bhuj, Okha, and Dwaraka, once the hallowed abode of Lord Krishna, and Gandhidham, a place no less sacred to millions of countrymen. Thousands of those poor, unfortunate who lost their all at the time of country's partition, took refuge at Gandhidham. The grim accounts of their suffering and deprivation rent her hearts.

The bridge at Kunverbet was being built over a creek of the sea. Most of the workers who came to work on this project were piece-rate workers. That is, the workers were paid according to the work done. They had come with the contractors on their own. They hailed mostly from the Ganjam district of Orissa and Kathghora in Madhya Pradesh. The old workers of the company were permanent in a sense. They had to shift from one branch of the company to another and change the sites too. The temporary or casual workers who were brought by the contractors had no guarantee of service. They were treated like old shoes. Their wages were very meagre although the contractors got huge amounts from the company on this count.

The life of extreme poverty that these labourers led slowly emerged clear to her. They were paid a mere pittance of Rs 3.50 for a day-long hard labour which included digging the soil, concrete mixing, sieving sand, oiling the cranes, lifting headloads of concrete mixture and reinforcement work like cutting and bending mild steel rods and the like.

One day, she saw a labourer slipped from a crane and fall upon a heap of iron forks. He was writhing and shrieking there in acute pain before being borne away to the company's hospital located in a that shed house. The old compounder declared that the man must be shifted to the Government hospital at Bhuj for proper treatment as his injuries were severe.

But Bhuj was three score miles away from Kunvarbet. Half of the road was *kachcha* (unasphalted). Madhu took the dying man in his own jeep to the hospital at Bhuj. Those were the bad days for her.

The Pakistani forces planned to blow up the bridge under construction. The atmosphere was tense. In such a situation, with Madhu away, she was sitting out of doors, anxious for him to return.

The convoys of the 'Jonga' jeeps of the Border Security Forces drove past her one after another along the road running past through the camp. She continued to sit there till past midnight. Gradually, a stillness descended upon the place, broken only by the throb of the stone crusher and the concrete vibrator at the worst site.

Distant shots at the border post reached her alert ears. But Madhu was not in sight! Her mind began to be panic.

The night watchman felt it advisable to say a word of warning : "The soldiers killed at the border are being taken along this way. Go and retire. Sirens will now sound for blackout. The company's generator will be switched off any moment. Better hurry up......"

She heard him but stood still. The 'Jonga' jeeps of the Army continued to roar past her one after another. But, all of a sudden, one of them braked to a halt at about eight yards from her, and two *jawans* in uniform jumped out of it. Their well-built forms were distinctly visible in the light of the vehicle. Terribly shaken, she rushed inside and bolted the door. After a while, she heard the whirr of the jeep driving away. Her heart shook with suspicion and fear. After years of agony and despair, she had just started breathing the new lease of life.

It was nearing daybreak when the distant sound of Madhu's jeep reached her eager ears. The next moment it arrived at the gate.

Greatly relieved, she opened the door to let him in. But, surprisingly, he would not have her in his loving arms that day as was his wont on other days. Blackout was sounded hours ago. In the dim light of a hurricane lamp, she saw his clothes all soiled and bloodstained. She grew nervous.

Sensing her fear, he said. "The poor fellow is dead. The police are yet to complete their report."

Towards morning she had a strange dream. She thought she saw a group of piece-rate workers advancing through the thorny bushes of the desert. But then the men assumed the forms of sheep. All of the desert strip and the work-site appeared to be carpeted with sheepskin. Each of the cacti that grew in the desert was changed into a sign of the cross. She felt perplexed for some time as to what the dream might signify, but forgot all about it soon after.

One day, she was surprised to find Madhu return abruptly from the work-site. He looked all harassed. To her inquiring look, he said without a prelude : "Listen, dear ! Hukum Singh, the crane driver, has been served a short notice. Another crane driver from some other branch has come here. He is armed with a note of recommendation from some high-ups."

Later she came to know that Hukum Singh, the crane driver from Gurdaspur, had once saved Madhu from the jaws of sure death. It was a Bholukdoba in Assam where they were both working on a bridge building project. As always, Madhu was the supervising engineer for the superstructure.

One day, as he was busy watching the crane lifting up heavy bundles of iron rods to the upper point of the bridge's framework, the load almost flew off the hook and was about to fall upon him when Hukum Singh, the operator, with rare presence of mind, swiftly swung the boom in the opposite direction and the bundle was found off at a distance upon a heap of sand. A terrible catastrophe was thus averted. Everybody around was astounded at Hukum Singh's alertness. And everybody was lavish in his praise. But now the same man had been treated by the company like a pair of worn-out shoes! No one would plead in Mr Singh's favour. None would help him to go to court to seek redress.

In 1965, the workers of this big construction company had no trade union for themselves. So, there was none to rend the air with loud words of protest against the dismissal of a skilled workman like Mr Singh. He came to bid her and Madhu goodbye.

He was sporting an unkempt beard. His shirt and pajamas were soiled. He had a bad cough. The sad turn of events for this innocent and luckless man sorely grieved my mind. So, he had to leave.

She saw him walking away with a tin trunk and a bedroll in hand until he was lost among the thorny desert bushes. It was an exciting time for her in the Rann of Kutch.

She discovered there afresh much of the grace and charm of life. In the desert tract of Kutch, a dust storm at night is a usual feature. They days are terribly hot but the nights are as cold as in winter.

6

Life in Vrindavan

It is only in a man's power to lead another from darkness to light. It is man alone who can bestow a new life upon another. For this, in love and understanding, lies the key.

She was awarded Sankardeva Scholarship to do research work at the Institute of Oriental Philosophy, Vrindaban, Uttar Pradesh. She acquired her Ph.D. degree in 1973 from Gauhati University for her thesis *Comparative Study of Goswami Tulsi Das's Ramcharita Manas and Madhava Kandali's Assamese Ramayana.*

She felt realised the truth of her remark when she was living alone in places like Kutch in Gujarat, Ahiron in Madhya Pradesh, the temple town of Vrindavan and in a 'barsati' on Roshanara Road, Delhi, and similar other places.

In August 1969, she started for Vrindavan. Her revered teacher, the late Upendra Chandra Lekharu had already sent her several letters and telegrams urging her to come there and take up research under his supervision. Her mind was deeply disturbed after Madhu's death. Someone seemed to whisper constantly in her ear : "Sitting idle like this with your soul benumbed. Pull yourself out of our gloom. March ahead. That way lied life."

The members of her family did not take kindly to her decision to go to Vrindavan. Her mother had, on her part, contacted one of her friends abroad to arrange to send her to London.

The mother must have thought that in London, in addition to pursuing her studies, she would come in contact with innumerable people, and that would provide a new spurt to the stagnant course of her life.

It was only after many years, in October 1986, to be precise, that she got a chance to visit London for a fairly long stay. She visited the city in the company of a businessman, Mr. Harbhajan Singh and his wife Mahindra.

All of them had taken their lodgings at Bucking Essex then. She was to have gone to that land of ancient Western tradition and culture about 20 years earlier. But it had so happened that instead of visiting London, she had gone to Vrindavan, the centre of ancient Hindu tradition and culture.

Her mind was in a turmoil after she had resigned her job at Goalpara Sainik School. To add to it, a few of our relatives, having learnt about her decision to go to Vrindavan added to her confusion.

They said : "It will be long before she completes her research at Vrindavan. How can she stay there for such a long? It's hardly wise that she should embark on this project."

Such unsolicited remarks depressed her mother heavily.

It was August. She got all her luggage ready. There being no girls' hostel available at Vrindavan, she was to arrange her own lodgings and cook her own meals.

As a result, there were quite a few things to carry, utensils included. Naturally, her luggage grew heavy.

On the day of her departure, her elder brother, who was then working at a place outside Guwahati, arrived home.

He checked her luggage and pulled out almost half of it as unnecessary.

"You will travel all by yourself with no one to help you. How can you carry such a mountain of luggage with you?" he said.

The luggage then was reduced in size and weight. Only the bare essentials were left.

Everyone felt that she was heading for an unknown future. Hence, all the members of the family were ready to bid her farewell with a heavy heart.

Many people known to her came to see her off at Guwahati railway station. They all looked very very sad.

She was all alone in a first class compartment. Of course, there were at times some short distance passengers, but they got down midway at their destinations.

In the morning, she discovered that she was all alone in the compartment. She felt so lonely.

She pulled the windows open and saw in the dim twilight a cluster of bare trees. It was perhaps at a point near about Siliguri.

A sense of acute agony almost tore her heart asunder. Each of the bare branches of the dew-soaked trees seemed to pierce her heart like sharp instruments of torture. There was no way she could console her mind. Where was she heading for? What was there in store for her? Why did Madhu leave her so suddenly?

She did not know anyone who grew so desperate. Even though badly mauled in life, they still continue to live. Her resolve never to yield to despair was now gone. Her eyes brimmed with tears.

The load of care on her mind grew heavy. There was no relief for her in sight. Thus she passed hard times prior to her research education in Vrindavan. Somehow she adjusted with the atmosphere of Vrindavan.

On October 20, 1970, her teacher and she were about to leave for the Institute. Just then the postman brought her a letter bearing the seal of the University of Delhi. She was asked to appear for an interview for the post of a lecturer in Assamese in the Department of Modern Indian Languages of the University.

It was in response to an application sent by her to the University from Guwahati about a year earlier on a brief visit to home. She had done it not out of her own will but at her mother's behest.

She was told that a lecturer's post was vacant in the department.

Seeing that her heart was not in the matter, the mother reproached her with lack of self-confidence.

"It's a pity you don't realise your capacity,"she often told her.

"My maternal uncle Mr. Subho Chandra Barua drafted the application, got it signed by me and posted it. I put the letter from the university in my purse."

Then my teacher remained pensive for a while. Then he said calmly : "Why should you feel so shy? All this is the will of the Lord. If appointed, the University will grant you leave to complete your work. Even if you don't get the job, you'll have no regrets, for the interview will be an experience for you."

Her teacher and she sat silently in a *tonga* which was fast moving towards the Institute.

She was in a pensive mood. Only the harsh clatter of the hoofs broke the noonday stillness.

She had never been organised person. She did not know how to keep her papers neatly. Those of her stories which were published in her school and college days were lost to her for she had not kept them vith care.

Her voluminous work, *Ramayana: From Ganga to Brahmaputra* is the output of her long research. It was published in 1996; released by the then President of India Dr. Shankar Dayal Sharma.

Having said that Dr Goswami is quite lucky to experience many interesting matters relating to social taboos and dogmas of the country.

7

Awards and Honours

> *I shall feel well-rewarded if the progeny reminisces of me as a humanist, asserts Dr Mamoni Raisom Goswami.*

She has received the International Tulsi Award on the occasion of International Conference on 'Tulsi Das and His Works,' from Florida International University, Florida, U.S.A. on November 20, 1999. Apart from this, Dr Goswami has been honoured with several awards:

1. Sahitya Academy Award in 1983, Delhi.
2. Assam Sahitya Sabha Award in 1988.
3. Bharat Nirman Award in 1989, Delhi.
4. Sauhardiya Award of Uttar Pradesh Hindi Sansthan in 1992, Lucknow.
5. Katha Award for Literature in 1993, Delhi.
6. Kamal Kumari Foundation Award in 1996.
7. International Jury's Award for the film *Adarya* based on her novel *Datal Hatir Unye Khowa Howda*. The film was directed by Dr. Shantana Bordoloi in 1997.
8. Jnanpith Award for the year 2000, Delhi.

Dr Goswami has been honoured by several institutions in India. Some of them are given below :

1. Manas Chatursadi Samittee, Delhi in 1978 for her works on Goswami Tulsi Das's *Ramcharita Manas* and Madhav Kandali's *Assamese Ramayana*.

2. Delhi Karnataka Sangha, with citation and a statue.
3. Assam Sahitya Sabha, on the occasion of their Silver Jubilee at Palasbari with a citation.
4. Assam Lekhika Samaroh with a citation.
5. Assam Lekhika Sanstha with a citation.
6. Assamese Department of Gauhati University with citation.
7. Merqhae Sahitya Sabha with citation.
8. Assam Foundation India with citation.

Besides these institutions, she has been honoured by various colleges and literary organisations with citations.

Dr Goswami has travelled widely via Europe, United Kingdom, Japan, other South East Asian countries and different states of India.

Jayanti Chattopadhaya, HOD, Department of MIL and Literary Studies, DU felicitated Dr Goswami at her department in 2001.

8

Member of Bodies

> *Dr. Goswami says, I am a crusader against female foeticide, girl child exploitation and all heinous crimes against women.*

Dr Indira Goswami is connected with a number of institutions and organisations. Some of them are:

1. The Advisory Committee (Assamese) of Sahitya Akademi, New Delhi (1988-93).
2. Member of Academic Council, Delhi University.
3. The Research Committee, Delhi University (1982-92).
4. The Arts Faculty, Delhi University (1989-92).
5. The Comparative Indian Literature Association, Delhi University.
6. The Board of Studies (Assamese), Banaras Hindu University.
7. Convenor of the Board of Studies (Assamese), Punjab Univesity (till 31st March 1993).
8. The Association of Indian Authors, New Delhi (1990-95).
9. Member of the Assamese Advisory Committee, National Book Trust of India, New Delhi.
10. Member of the Governing Body of Miranda House, University of Delhi.
11. Member of the College of Arts, Delhi University.

their remaining years in the holy city of Vrindaban, in the hope of 'mukti' and salvation.

Dantal Hatir Une Khowa Howda (1988, *The Worm-eaten Howda of a Tuskar*): She received the prestigious Assam Sahitya Sabha Award for this novel. This is a powerful novel which has been listed as a masterpiece of Indian Literature by both Sahitya Akademi and National Book Trust of India (in the book, Masterpieces of Indian Literature, Volume I). The setting is a *Sattra* (Vaisnavite monastic institute of Assam) in the South Kamrup District of Assam. The plot revolves around the lives of three Brahmin widows in the family of Sattra Adhikar (head of the monastic institute). The theme is the socio-economic decadence of the feudal institute lingering on till the modern times on the threshold of Independence of India, and the repression of widows in orthodox Brahmin society. The feature film in Assamese based on this novel won several national and international awards.

Tez Aru Dhulire Dhusarita Pristha (1995, *Pages Soiled With Blood and Dust*): This novel is based on the political violence and social unrest in the city of Delhi, amidst the communal riots that broke out in the aftermath of Indira Gandhi's assassination. It is in the form of a diary of a woman protagonist. living alone in Delhi, and recording her first-hand experiences during the riots in 1984.

Nangotha Shahar (Naked City): In this novel, she has tried through the main character to express the agony of being lonely even when surrounded by friends, elders and others.

10

Published Works

> *Dr. Goswami says, Writing is in my blood, in my veins. If I stop I will die of suffocation. Without my pen I will die...... Without my pen I will die...... With my writings I am free as a bird, to fly anywhere to be anyone, to understand anything.*

1. ***Chinaki Mamoni*** (A collection of short stories), Guwahati : Lawyers Book Stall, 1962.
2. ***Kaina*** (A collection of short stories), Guwahati : Dutta Barua and Company, 1966.
3. ***Hridaya ek Nadirnam*** (A collection of short stories), Guwahati : Sahitya Prakashan, Tribune Group of Publishers, 1st edition, 1990; 2nd edition, 1991 and 3rd edition, 1995.
4. ***Nirbachita Galpa*** (A collection of short stories), New Delhi : National Book Trust of India, 1998.
5. ***Nirbachita Galpa*** (A collection of stories), Hindi Translation of Short Stories.
6. ***Priya Galpa*** (A collection of short stories) Guwahati : Jyoti Prakashan, 1999.
7. ***Chenabar Srata*** (novel), Guwahati : Lawyers Book Stll, 1972, 2nd edition, 1999.
8. ***Neel Kanthi Braja*** (novel), Guwahati : Lawyers Book Stall, 1st edition, 1972; 2nd edition, 1988; 3rd edition, 1990; 4th edition, 1998.
9. ***Neel Kanthi Braja*** (translated into Hindi by Dr. R.N.Tripathi) Delhi, Janapriya Publications, 1998.

10. ***Ahiron*** (novel), Guwahati : 1st publication, 1980 by Bani Prakash, Guwahati; 2nd edition, Guwahati : Students Stores, 1988; 3rd edition, 1990; 4th edition, 1993 and 5th edition, 1993.

11. ***Mamare Dhara Tarowal Aru Dukhan Upanyas*** (*Nagnath Shahar, Budha Sagar, Dhusar Gaisa Aru Mahamad Musa*), Guwahati : Saraighat Printers, 1st edition,1980; 2nd edition, Guwahati : Dutta Barua And Co., 1984; 3rd edition, Guwahati : Lawyers Book Stall, 1992.

    [NB : Dr Goswami received Sahitya Akademy Award for 1982 for the above mentioned novel]

12. ***Marche Dhara Tarowal*** (Bengali translation of *Marare Dhara Tarowal*), New Delhi : Sahitya Akademy, 1998.

13. ***Une Khowa Hawda*** (Novel), Guwahati: Bani Prakash, 1st edition, 1988; 2nd edition, 1992; 3rd edition, 1996 and 4th edition, 1996.

    [NB: Dr Goswami received the prestigious Sahitya Sabha Award for the book.]

14. ***Saga of South Kamrup*** (English translation of *Une Khowa Howda*), New Delhi : Sahitya Akademy, 1998.

15. ***Dakshini Kamrup Ki Gatha*** (Hindi translation of *Une Khowa Howda*) New Delhi : Sahitya Akademy, 1997.

16. ***Adha Lekha Dastavej*** (Autobiography of Dr. Indira Goswami), Guwahati : Students Stores, 1st edition, 1988; 2nd edition, 1990, 3rd edition, 1995 and 4th edition, 1998.

17. ***Ardhavritta Jivanyatra*** (Nepali translation of ***Adha Lekha Dastavej***) Darjelling: Shyam Prakashan.

    [NB: This translation was awarded Sahitya Akademi Award for translation for the year 1999].

18. ***Jivan Koi Sauda Nahin*** (Hindi translation of ***Adha Lekha Dastavej*** by Neeta Banarjee) Delhi : Hind Pocket Book Ltd., 1st and 2nd editions.

19. ***Sanskar, Udaybharnur Chaitra Etayadi*** (A collection of novels) Kolkata: Sreebhumi Publisher, 1st edition, 1989 and 2nd

edition, 1990; 3rd and 4th editions, Guwahati : Students Stores, 1993 and 1995. It is a collection of three novels.

20. ***Mahijoshi Kamala*** (autobiographical novel) Guwahati : Chandra Prakash, 1997.
21. ***Upanayas Samagra*** (Collection of Novels) Guwahati : Students Stores, 1998.
22. ***Dasarathar Putrar Khoj*** (novel) Guwahati : Bani Prakash, 1999.
23. (a) ***Iswari Jakhami Jatri Aru Anyana Yatra*** (This collection has one more novel and a short story.)

    (b) ***Eswari Jakhmi Yatri*** [both these novels and the short story were published under the *Iswari Jakhmi Uatri Aru Ananya Yatra*.]
24. ***Ramayana: From Ganga to Brahmaputra*** (A critical work) B.R. Publisher, Delhi.
25. ***Premchander Choti Galpa*** (autology of Munshi Premchand's short stories) New Delhi : National Book Trust of India, 1st edition, 1975; 2nd edition, 1988; 3rd edition, 1990 and 4th edition, 1998.
26. ***Adha Ghanta Samaya*** (translation of Malayalam novel *Aranazhika Neram*) New Delhi : National Book Trust of India, 1st edition, 1978 and 2nd edition, 1998.
27. ***Kalam*** (a collection of Hindi, Urdu, Punjabi and Bengali short stories), translated by Dr Goswami and Smt. Papari Goswami published by Students Stores, Guwahati.
28. ***Sarisnipar Katha*** (translation of a Japanese book *Sarisnipar Sakulo* by Shriji Tajima and Kang Woo, Hyon), published with support from the Toyota Foundation, Tokyo through Nandartha, New Delhi.
29. ***Ahnik*** (it is a translation of Oriya award winning collection of poems by J.P. Das and published by Sahitya Akademy, New Delhi.
30. ***Jatak Katha*** (anthology of the stories of Jatak), published by Publication Division, Government of India.

31. ***The Fictional World of Indira Goswami,*** published by B.R. Publicaton, Delhi.
32. ***Chinnamosta*** *(a novel on balipratha)*
33. ***The Shadow of Kamakhya*** (2002).

Dr. Goswami is one of the scholars associated with the History of Indian Literature, Volume VII and Volume VIII edited by Professor S.K.Das, published by Sahitya Akademy, New Delhi, 1993 and 1995 respectively.

Short Stories of Dr Goswami are included in the following anthologies and journals:

Modern Indian Short Stories, Vol.4, 1983, published by Indian Council for Cultural Relations, New Delhi.

Indian Love Stories, edited by Sudhir Kakar, Delhi : Lotus Collection, Roli Books, 1999.

Imagining The Others, edited by Sara Rai, pulished by Katha, May 1999.

Indian Literature, No.112, No.181, published by Sahitya Akademy, New Delhi in 1986 and 1989 rspectively.

Samkalin Bharatiya Sahitya, Vol.36, published by Sahitya Akademy, New Delhi, April-June 1981.

Glimpses : TheModern Indian Short Story, published by East West Press Ltd., New Delhi, 1992.

The State of Life : An anthology of stories by Indian Women, published by Kali for Women, New Delhi, 1992.

Savvy Collection of Indian Short Stories, published by Arnold, 1992.

Indian Perspective, printed and published for the Ministry of External Affairs, Government of India, New Delhi, 1991.

Katha, Prize Stories, Vol.3. the best short stories published during 1991-93 in eleven Indian Languages by Katha Publications, New Delhi.

Separate Journeys, short stories by Indian writers), published by Mantra Publishing Ltd. first published in Great Britain in 1993.

Samadarshi, publishes by Punjabi Akademy, New Delhi, 1999.

Samakalin Bharatiya Sahitya published by Sahitya Akademy in July, 2000.

Indian Literature (women writers special issue) published by Sahitya Akdemy, New Delhi.

Women (a collection of Assamese short stories) published on the occasion of diamond jubilee celebration of Handique Girls' College, Guwahati, 1999).

Besides the above mentioned collections, Dr. Indira Goswami's stories have been published in Assamese anthologies like *Asomiya Premar Galpa, Basarar Shreshtha Galpa* and many others. Her stories have also appeared in other Indian languages in the special issues of *Andhra Prabha* (Telugu), *Gujjar Bharati* (Gujarati), *Mathrubhumi* (Malayalam), etc. Several books have been written on the life and works of Indira Goswami so far. Some of them are:

Hridayar Tapashvini, edited by Rani Gohain, Jyoti Prakash, Guwahati.

Critical Study of the Writings of Indira Goswami by Malaya Khaund, B.R. Publication, New Delhi.

Mamoni Raisom Swapna-Duswaphar Diary, edited by Hemanta Kumar Bharali, published by Chitralekha Publications, Guwahati.

Indira Goswami (Mamoni Raisom Goswami) as Indian author and her works, published by B.R. Publication.

11

Research Articles

Dr. Goswami says, I don't care as I write whatever I feel is ethically correct.

There are a good number of research papers of Dr. Goswami. Some of the published papers are given below :

Madhava Kandali's Ramayana and Contemporary Society, Journal of the University of Gauhati, Vol.XXIV-XXV, No.1 Arts, 1973-74.

Kandali's Assamese Ramayana and Tulsi's Ramcharita Manas, Journal of the Assam Research Society, Guwahati, Assam, Vol.XXIII, 1977-78.

Treatment of Ravana in the Hands of the Assamese Poet, Madhava Kandali and Goswami Tulsi Das, Souvenir of Assam Association Silver Jubilee Volume, 1975.

Children's Literature in the Assamese Language, Delhi, Ministry of Information and Broadcasting, Publication Division, 1982.

Birendra Kumar Bhattacharya's Novel, Mrityunjay, Samakalin Bharatiya Sahitya, Sahitya Akademy, New Delhi, Vol.XVIII, 1984.

History of Assamese Literature, Chudar, Delhi Tamil Sangam, Vol.XXVII, 1974.

Madhava Kandali and His Ramayana, published by All India Oriental Conference, Volume of 27th session, 1974.

Assamese Literature Since 1974, Indian and Foreign Review, Ministry of Information and Broadcasting, Vol.XV, No.5, 15 December 1975.

Assamese Metres, published by University Book Production Board, Ahmedabad, Gujarat, 1975.

Assamese drama : Modernity without vitality, The Hisdustan Times, November 20, 1977.

Ramabhakti in Sankara Deva, published by Sri Sankara Deva Institute of Oriental Culture, New Delhi, on the occasion of 527th Birth Anniversary of Mahapurusha Sankara Deva, October 27, 1975.

Chronicle of a Great Woman, Indian Literature, May-June 1992.

About twenty articles have been published on various subjects of art and culture of Assam, including the study of Belur and Halebi, Dwarka temples, etc. in Assamese papers like *Asom Bani*, *Dainik Asom*, *Saptahik Nilachal* and so on .

Ankianats of Assam, Deepika, Journal of Oriya Department, Vishwa Bharati, Shantiniketan, Vol.XII, 1981.

I and My Writing, published by the Department of Modern Indian Laguages and Literary Studies, University of Delhi.

Portrayal of Ravana in Ramacharita Manas and Kandali's Ramayana, published by Digboi College, Silver Jubilee Celebration Souvenir, Digboi, Assam, 1990-91.

The Image of Women in Assamese Literature, published in *The Image of Women in Indian Literature*, edited by Yashoda Bhat and Yamuna Raja Rao, B.R. Publishing Corporation, Delhi. This paper was presented by a noted scholar at a national seminar organised by N.K.K.R.V. College for Women, Bangalore.

Ravana in Kandali's Assamese Ramayana and Tulsi's Ramcharia Manas, published in the Souvenir of 8th International

Ramayana Conference, University of Leuven, Belgium, held from July 6 to 8, 1991. Dr Goswami participated in the conference and presented the above paper.

Comparative study of the characters of Ravana and Sita, published in the souvenir of 11th International Ramayana Conference, held in Thammasat University, Thailand on December 15 to 17, 1994.

Bani Kanta Kakati, published in the souvenir of centenary celebration of Bani Kanta Kakati held in the Departmant of Modern Indian Languages and Literary Studies, University of Delhi, from March 1 to 3, 1995.

Cherished Memories of T.C. Girls High School, published in the golden jubilee volume of T.C. Girls High School on 19-20-21 September 1995.

Maheshwar Neog : Some Cherished Memories, published in commemorative volume on Dr. Neog, published by Dr. M. Neog Trust, Guwahati, September 7, 1995.

Assamese Literature on Freedom Movement in the Constitution of Indian literature towards the freedom movement in India 1900-1947, published by Central Secretariat Library, Ministry of Culture and Youths Affairs, New Delhi.

Besides these articles, many articles of Dr Goswami have been published in *The Hindustan Times, Natun Asamiya, Saptahik Hindustan, Cottonian,* etc.

Several feature films, TV serials, telefilms and stage plays have been based on Indira Goswami's novels and short stories.

12

Seminars and Papers

> *Dr. Goswami says, It's true that authors cannot show humanity a concrete route for a change, but they can definitely make them realise their own naked reality and situations.*

Some national and international seminars in which Dr. Goswami participated are as follows:

Ramayana of Madhava Kandali, a paper read in All India Oriental Conference held at Kurukshetra, Haryana, 1974.

Two papers read in the National Conference of Ramayana in 1974 and 1983, held at Chitrakuta, Madhya Pradesh.

A paper on *Ankiya Nats of Assam* was read in the national seminar on Oriya literature organised by Vishwa Bharati University in 1981.

A paper on Assamese literature was read in the Writers' Conference held at Balagir, Orissa in 1987.

She read a paper in the national seminar on Ramayana trdition, Raj Bhavan, Patna, Bihar on August 12, 1986.

Read a paper on *Aim and Struggle of Women Writers*, in the National Conference on Women Writers held at Guwahati, Assam, under the sponsorship of Lekhika Sanstha of Assam.

Read a paper on *The Role of Women Writers* in the national seminar held in New Delhi and organised by Sahitya Akademy,

New Delhi, and the Deprtment of Women's Welfare in December, 1986.

Read a paper on *Freedom Struggle in Assam* for Nikhil Bharat Banga Sahitya Sammelan, New Delhi on December 25, 1987.

Read a paper on *Assamese prose literature* in a national seminar held in Janaki Devi Mahavidyalaya of Delhi University on CCHSSIP Scheme on March 19, 1990.

Read a paper on *Assamese-Bengali Relation* in the Akhil Banga Sahitya Sanmilan (held in connection with 300 years of Kolkata) in Kolkata in October, 1990.

Delivered lectures in Dibrugarh University on refresher courses in Assamese department from November 8 to 10, 1991. Two lectures were delivered on the Ramayani literature and one of her own writing.

Invited by India International Centre and Sahitya Akademy to speak in their programme, *Meet the Author*, in the Auditorium of India International Centre, New Delhi on November 1, 1992.

Read a paper on *Fakir Mohan Senpati and Harakanta Sadarmin* in the national seminar held on Fakir Mohan Senapati by the Department of Modern Indian Languages and Literary Studies, University of Delhi in 1993.

Delivered a keynote address in the Department of Modern Indian Languages and Literary Studies, University of Delhi in their seminar on Women Writers of Medieval India, sponsored jointly by Kannada Languages Wing and Kannada Sangh of Delhi in 1992.

Delivered a lecture and presided over a session in the natioanl seminar organised by N.M.K.R.V. College for Women, Bangalore on the subject of Indian literature in 1992 in Karnataka.

Read a paper on *Role of Women* in the All India Women Conference held at Dibrugarh, Assam.

Went as Chief Guest to Calcutta Book Fair, 1991 and read a paper on her own writings at a function held in Calcutta. She presided over all Assam Women Conference held at Nazira on Janurary 3, 1994.

Went as one of the Chief Guests in National Lietrary Seminar, from December 17 to 20, 1994 in Kerala.

Went to preside over one session of the seminar on *Non-natives in Indian Literature* held in Karnataka Bhavan, Delhi, 1996.

Delivered *The Hemanta Kumar Sharma Memorial Licture* in Cotton College, affiliated to Gauhati Uniersity in March 1996.

Went as the Chief Guest to the Golden Jubilee Celebration of Darrang College, Tezpur, on November 16, 1997.

Read a paper on *Fakir Mohan Senapati and Contemporary Indian Fiction* in the national seminar orgnised by Sahitya Akademy, Delhi on January 14 and 16, 1994.

Read the keynote paper on a seminar organised by Bengali Department at Miranda House, Delhi University, 1995.

Read a paper in the national seminar on *Traditional Influences on Indian Society* organised by Kalaikoodam in collaboration with India International Centre, Delhi on 25 and 26 October 1997.

Went as the Chief Guest to the felicitation programme on National Poet Shailendra Sharma in Hyderabad, 15 October 1997.

Read a paper and went as the Chief Guest in the national seminar orgnised by Srimanta Sankar Dev Sangha on the occasion of 550th Birth Anniversary of Srimanta Sankar Deka held at Vithal Bhai Patel Bhavan, New Delhi on October 1, 1998.

Went as a Chief Guest, and read a paper on Dalit Literature in Kerala Sahitya Akademi, at Town HallThrissur on December 26, 1996.

Invited by Sahitya Sabha to speak in *Meet the Author* programme in Sahitya Sabha Bhavan, Guwahati, July, 1993.

Read a paper on *Sanskrit studies in Assam*, and Assamese Ramayana in the national seminar on Sanskrit and Indian Language.

Presided over the Annual Conference of Lekhika Samaroh Samity held at Janji, 1997.

Attended several conferences of Lekhika Samaroh and Lekhika Samstha, Assam as a Speaker.

Besides these, several papers have been read in national seminar on Indian literature.

Assamese Ramayana of 14th Century - Its Poetic Beauty and Novelty, a paper read in the international seminar on Ramayana Tradition and National Cultures in Asia, organised by Cultural Affairs Department, Government of Uttar Pradesh, at Lucknow in October 1986.

Writer in Freedom Struggle of India, this paper was read in the international seminar held in New Delhi and organised by Bulgarian Information Centre, in December.

Madhava Kandali's Assamese Ramayana and Ramcharit Manas, this paper was read in 4th International Conference on Ramayana held in Vigyan Bhavan, New Delhi on 20th December 1988.

Assamese Language and the Language of Ramayana, a paper which was read in a symposium on language and linguistics held in Faculty of Liberal Arts (Thammsat University, Bangkok, Thailand in June, 1988).

Renovations of the Ramayana of North-East India, a paper read in the 5th International Ramayana Conference held in Janakpur (Nepal) in 1988.

Hindu Society in Ramayana Literature of North-East India, a paper read in the 6th International Ramayana Conference held in Mauritius from August 8 to 15, 1990.

A paper on *The Characters of Ramayana* was presented by Dr. Goswami in the 8th International Conference held in Louven University of Belgium from July 6 to 8, 1991. She had chaired one of the sessions of this conference.

A paper on the illustrated manuscripts of *Ramcharita Manas* and the Assamese Ramayana was read in the 9th International Conference on Ramayana, held at Denpasar, Bali (Indonesia) from 5th to 9th July 1992.

Went to Mauritius as a Government delegate to Vishwa Hindi Sammelan held from December 2 to 4, 1993.

Vice-chaired a session in the 11th International Ramayana Conference held in Thailand from December 15 to 17, 1994.

Chaired a session in the 13th International Ramayana Conference held in Shenjhen University, China.

Chaired a session on the International Seminar on Ghalibs Worlds, Tunes, Ideas and Contemporaries on the occasion of the bi-centenary of Mirza Ghalib at India International Centre from December 14 to 16 , 1998 organised by Sahitya Akademy and Urdu Akademy.

Chaired over a session in the 15th International Conference on Ramayana held in Port of Spain (Trinid) on August 2, 1998.

Read a keynote paper on the 1st International Conference on Ramayana and Mahabharata held at Malaysia University, Kuala Lampur, Malaysia, from October 21 to 24, 1999.

Chaired a session in the International Seminar of Ghalib organised by Sahitya Akademy and Urdu Akademy in Delhi on July 13, 1999.

Chaired a session in the International Conference on Tulsidas and His Works at Florida International University, Miami, U.S.A.

Dr. Goswami was given the International Tulsi Award in this Conference on November 26, 1999.

"Madhava Kandali's Assamese Ramayana and Ramcharit Manas" — this paper was read in the 4th International Conference on Ramayana held in Vigyan Bhavan, New Delhi on December 20, 1988.

"Assamese Language and the Language of Ramayana" is read in the symposium on language and linguistics held in Faculty of Liberal Arts (Thammsat University, Bangkok, Thailand in June 1988).

"Hindu Society in Ramayana Literature of North East India," a paper read in the 6th International Ramayana Conference held in Mauritius from August 8 to 15, 1990.

The paper on "The Characters of Ramayana", depicted by the poets of Northeast India and in Hindi belt, was presented in the 8th International Conference held in Louven University of Belgium from July 6 to 8, 1991. She had chaired one of the sessions of this conference. Thus, besides these international seminars, she presented and read papers in several seminars and conferences all over India.

Noted dancer Uma Sarma, Dr Goswami, Dongri writer Padma Shasri and English writer Aruna Vasudeva met in Delhi in 2001.

13

Guiding Research Works

> *My introspective spirit has provoked me to protest against the unjust animal sacrifice system in Assam in Chinnamosta, says Dr Mamoni Raisom Goswami*

Dr. Goswami guided a good number of students for their Ph.D. theses and M.Phil dessertations. Some of them are as follows :

1. Mr. Kanan Mishra of Orissa for his dissertation on *Treatment of Nature, by Raghunath Choudhury of Assam and Nandkishore of Orissa.*
2. Mr. Mohini Kumar Bordoloi of Assam on *A comparative study of two novels : Mrinalini of Bengal and Dandua Droh of Assam.*
3. Ms. Seema Suneel of Delhi on *Man and Woman Relations in the Assamese Novel: A tale of nomadic soul (Aghari Atmar Kahini) and the Hindi novel, Machli Bazar.*
4. Ms. Malaya Khound of Assam awarded Ph.D. degree on the topic *Birendra Kumar Bhattacharya and His Works.*
5. Ph.D. thesis of Dr. Suman Bala of Delhi is in progress on the topic *Gandhi and the Indian Fiction.*
6. Ph.D. thesis of Smt. Rejina Begam is in progress. Her topic is *Hitesh Deka and his works.*

14

Remarks on Her Works

Dr. Goswami says: I observe people, analyse them and put it down on paper. It comes naturally.

Different quarters have treated the literary works of Dr Goswami differently. Some of the remarks about her writings by different scholars, national newspapers and others are stated below:

The greatest woman novelist in Assam

"Acclaimed as perhaps the greatest woman novelist in Assam today."

— ***Masterpieces of Indian Literature***, Volume I, published by National Book Trust of India, Page-9

"Through Indira Goswami's stories the North-east comes to the literary mainstream."

—**"Urvashi Butalia"**, Hindustan Times, 27.1.2002

❀ ❀ ❀ ❀ ❀

A stern out-cry of realism

"After reading Mamoni Raisom Goswami's (Indira Goswami's) *Mamare Dhara Tarowal*, I heard a stern out-cry of realism, aching in my ears. The picture of the stern realism and non-Cathertic atmosphere is also a novel creation. I read it long ago but I still remember these tortured images."

— Birendra Kumar Bhattacharya.

❀ ❀ ❀ ❀ ❀

Rare soul

"Indira Goswami is one of those rare souls who have been able to get an insight into the great power which is behind this universe. In turn, the endeavour to grapple with that power finds reflection in this book and lends strength to it..... This power that this metamorphosis has bestowed upon her has now become a matter of pride for every Assamese woman."

— Amrita Pritam, on the preface of *Indira Goswamis's An Unfinished Autobiography*

❀ ❀ ❀ ❀ ❀

Extraordinary author

"Mamoni Raisom Goswami is the most extraordinary thing to have happened to Assamese literature in recent years. She has sprung upon her readers a whole new world of experience — feelings, perceptions, thoughts, character, types and situationas — that amaze and enthrall..... A singular intensity of feeling and a searching honesty, courage, and masterful confidence of expression mark her writings...... When the products of her several years reached the reading public, they were astouneded by her phenomenal sensitivensess and the range and depth of her imaginative vision. Her language combines remarkable economy with passion and sensuous vigour, realised with telling details. There cannot be any doubt that she is a major author from whom great things can be expected.

-Dr. Hiren Gohain

In search of a new horizon

"I have the pleasure and previledge to talk a few words about our dearest colleague Indira Goswami, while felicitating her for the grand achievement of getting the most prestigious literary award of the country, viz. the Jnanapeeth Award.

Before the advent of Indira, Assamese novel was marred by artificial sentimental dialogues and direct simple narration. Indira contributed it with the natural dialogues, intensity of subjective experience and creative imagery.

Let me share with you my own experience of Indira's creative process. Seven years before, when I was invited to deliver a memorial lecture at the famous Cotton College, I was travelling in a car from Guwahati to the Kaziranga National Park; and Indira was accompanying me. We were rather running late in our schedule and were worried to reach the wild forest before dark. Suddenly our car broke down at a remote place and it was revealed that it would take a couple of hours to get it going. So Indira and I ventured to a road-side dhaba to have a drink of tender coconut. A fragile old man with a smiling face attended to us. Indira soon got busy in intimate conversation with him. The man also obliged us by singing a couple of Shankardev's devotional songs on the tune of his dotara. We resumed to our further journey when the car was okay. That was an experience. Next day Indira told me that she was writing a short story on that experience. After about a year I came across the English translation of that story when it was awarded and published by 'Katha'. And my God! What a creative change that experience had got in the story! Indira has retained me as a character in that story, but my nature is totally changed. I am portrayed a constantly scared of Assam-terrorists. But that is not the main thing. Some indegenous characters have entered the story, which were not there in the actual experience. The old man of the story is accompanied by his wife, who gives a contrasting just a position to his smiling & pleasant personality by her constant worries about their son, who had been lived away by terrorists. Then there is a daughter of the couple, who had fallen in love with an Army-jawan and was beaten mercilessly for that reason by her brother. I (in the story) give sumptuous money to the old man for his services, and suddenly his terrorist son appears from nowhere and grabs the money, with the intention of purchasing arms from the poachers. Indira had, with a magic touch of literary creativity, intermingled threads of information and happenings which she had collected during the conversation with the old man, and interwoven a dramatic story!

This fact of intermingling real subjective experience with keen observation and susceptible empathy is the core of Indira's literary creativity. In her two novels *Chenabar Shrota* and *Ahiron*, she has portrayed lives and problems of workers at the bridge construction work. These were her sympathetic observations during her own stay at such sites with her late engineer husband. In *Neelakanthi Vraj* she presents pathetic portraits of neglected widows and old people dying at road-side, which she had observed during her own stay at Vrindavan.

Dotal Hatir Unye Khowa Howda is a masterpiece not only among Indira's novels, but in the Indian novel as well. The title of this novel itself a very powerful image. It means, the moth-eaten Howda of a tusker, and it presents the image of a drudalistic 'Satra', which was glorious at a time in the past, but which has reached a pathetic condition of existance now. This novel revolves round three widows of the Gosain family, Durga, Soru and Giribala. Durga is the eldest of the three. Her portrait bears shadows of darkness and death. Giribala is the youngest. She cannot accept the bondages and restrictions imposed upon widows by the society. She rebels against them. Soru Gosain is extremely sensitive, humane and delicate. She is standing between the old world of Durga and the new world of Giribala and oscillating towards the two. Indira has depicted the agony of the devastating old family system very sympathetically in this novel.

The world of Indira's short stories is also rich with a variety of experiences. One of her powerful short stories presents the portrait of a Brahmin prostitute, who gives her flesh to a person of a low caste, in order to extinguish the fire of hunger, but refuses to sow the seed of his child in her body. The range of human experiences in her short stories varies from the lives of people living near a funeral ground, whose occupation is to cremate the dead bodies and sell their own flesh, to the sophisticated and elite lives of university professors. Whatever she observes, she combines it with creative imagination and brings out in the form of a short story.

I congratulate Indira for her tremendous success in the field of creative literature and sincerely wish that many more such honours come to her in future."

Prof. N.D.Mirajkar
(Talk at the function of felicitation of Indira Goswami in the Department of Modern Indian Languages & Literary Studies, Delhi University, Delhi, on August 23, 2001).

❀ ❀ ❀ ❀ ❀

Artistic control

"*An Unfinished Autobiography* is remarkable for its quality and tone, exuding a quiet courage in the way it expounds the sensitive reactions of an educated critical woman of those times. It shows not only the orgnic growth of a writer, but also the strain under which a writer lives. With writers like Goswami firmly entrenched in her roots, we reach a writing that goes far beyond the mere niceties of language to a reality that is direct and uncultured. For instance, Goswami's authorial poise in rendering some of the stubborn patterns in a structured society - like Brahmanian that practises cruel rituals on women, particularly widowed women, shows a tight artistic control, giving an authentic account of a decadent section of civilisation. Her strength here is partly drawn from a certain mode of 'realism' however wary one has grown of this term in the light of recent critical sophistications of truth. This explains the commendable absence of a shrill voice even when the author notes some outrageous indignities against women in an apparently impersonal way. Perhaps, it is this distance in combination with her mooring that gives her the clarity of perspective to see the flaw of her society. The entire exercise of her authobiography makes for a good foil for her fiction. Sizing up a different life on the terms lived she displays the same mereless gap in dealing with the events in her own life, as she did in her fiction."

— Comments on *Selected Works of Indira Goswami* in *The Times of India*, Feb 26, 1989

❀ ❀ ❀ ❀ ❀

A creative fiction

"*Selected Works of Indira Goswami* undoubtedly falls into the category of creative fiction. This is because Indira Goswami chooses to confront real, pulsating life, in all its baffling complexity.

In her novel, there is no manipulation, no endeavour to establish any palpable ideology, Her imagination is charged with humanism only. Even when she exposes hypocrisy, orthodoxy or corruption, there is no anger — only compassion, empathy and understanding. Maybe this is because her sensibility, which is basically poetic, uses metaphors and similes to articulate those nuances of emotion which are often intractable to prose.

But the novel that shows her creative versatility and technical virtuosity is Ahiron. This novel generates tension through an interplay of contrasted values and characters. Here Indira Goswami seems to evoke all the five senses, particularly the sense of smell. Even the honey hat that flows from the life of another man's wife is compared to the odour of a garland of *Chameli*. Indira Goswami's fiction is pure art unencumbered with social, political or religious ethoes."

— Comments on *Selected Works of Indira Goswami* by Shiv K. Kumar in *Hindustan Times*

A phoenix

"She would like to change the world — this man's world to a luminous, harmonious place. More than two dozen novels and one autobiography in their fictional, engrossing style convey the same message.

But like a phoenix, Indira .... writer fictionalising the experiences of bliss and blessedness, her sorrow and bitterness. Literature was her refuge, writing was her new passion.

Indira comfortably weaves fascinating novels against backdrops of human deprivations, exploitation of the weak and laces them with revolutionary ideology for sweeping away the decadent and the destructive and ushering in the emancipated human being."

— Interview with Indira Goswami
in *Sunday Herald,* May 27, 1990.

❀ ❀ ❀ ❀ ❀

Struggling shadows

"Dr. Goswami succeeds in portraying the contradictions from within a society that has become stagnant in its refusal to move forward. *Shadow of Dark God* captures the images of a dark and bright world in which men and women exist as shadows struggling hopelessly for their mere survival ....

The significance of the novel lies in the fact that the tormentor is not condemned, but both the oppressor and the oppressed are shown as victims of a mindless system. The author neither exhibits her anger against or sympathy for any one concerned, which makes this work a pure work of art.

— Comments of *Shadow of Dark God and the Sin* by
Indira Parthasarthy in *The Hindu,* March 23, 1987

A panoromic view

The novel is a panoramic view of the Hindu mythology and psyche rooted in the hallowed ground of Vrindaban. It is an overwhelming exposition of pristine and pure love, reverential man-god relationship and the bestial religious, spiritual exploitation of the unfortunate destitue, the gulliu but the faithful... Surprisingly, the appended short story (Offspring) helps to heighten the effect of the novel rather than drag on it.

(Comments on Shadow of Dark God and the Sin by Raj Gill in Hindustan Times, November, 29, 1987)

❀ ❀ ❀ ❀ ❀

Insearch of a velvet dress

For Indira Goswami, the Assamese writer who won the Sahitya Akademi Award in 1982, language is like a velvet dress with which she tried to cover the restless soul as it lives out its life. But sometimes she feels it is futile to try and arrest the soul in the cold print of language: would it not be better simply to experience life in dumb silence?

Try as she might, she unloads her psyche and through her creative efforts weaves the dress, she finds that it is made not of velvet, not even fine muslin; it is tattered fabric, but with a beauty which puts the finest velvets to shame.

A kind of morbid feeling has haunted her all her life, and her own personal sufferings are depicted through the sufferings of her characters, with whom she identifies. In the novel *Naked City*, she has tried through the main character to express the agony of being lonely even when surrounded by friends, elders and others.

All the novels have been based on actual experiences and for many she has drawn inspiration from real life people. However, she has not written a novel which has given her complete satisfaction. She is still in search of the velvet dress which will capture the soul, but finds that her heroines, like Cinderalla at the midnight crime, find themselves dressed in tattered dress, and for them there is no easy escape from a prince. They often find a harder way out, like Giribala, the progagonist in one of her novels, who is unable to fight the social taboos and commits suicide."

— *The Statesmen*, December 31, 1986

Great creative literature

"Mamoni Goswami has earned for herself a distinctive place among Assamese writers. She has extended the horizon of Assamese novels through unusually fresh subjects and backgrounds. The theme of the novel *Ahiron* revolves around the life of a group of different categories of employees and labourers serving under a company engaged in the cinstruction of a aqueduct on river *Ahiron* in Madhya Pradesh and a woman who came in contact with them. The writer has scanned the characters of the engineers, the clerks, the cook, the washerman, the driver, the labourers as well as of the women with an outlook that is totally humane. The other characters with all the earthly virtues and weaknesses, which fit into the story, have also come up alive in the competent hands of the writer.

She has succeeded in creating a deep impact in the readers' mind through natural conversation, bits of feedback and imageries created with relatively fewer words as against artificial emotional dialouge and direct narrations that are generally noticed in Assamese novels. The other notable element is the attractive style of story telling. However, the qualities that have made the novel nobler are the writer's natural sympathy, generosity and deep understanding of life. The inter-personal understanding and love and affection that survive death seem to be the central theme of the novel. The significance of a novel that carries such a message against the cruel setting of strangulated humanism and humanity in the modern age cannot be gain said.

In spite of some shortcomings like use of crude language, repetition of similies and a few errors, due to oversight, of thematic incoherence, Mamoni Raisom Goswami's latest novel *Ahiron* is a significant contribution to Assamese literature. This short novel has also the elements of great creative literature."

— Review of *Ahiron* by Padum Baruah in *Pratinidihi*, December, 1983

❀ ❀ ❀ ❀ ❀

Novelty of themes

"Mamoni Raisom Goswami is a familiar name in the Assamese literary world. Smt. Goswami's writings are marked by the novelty of themes and distinct style of expression. She has exposed the Assamese readers to the varied experience she had gathered while staying at different places outside Assam. She has projected in the writings actual experiences of city life. The life of labourers and also the peculiar environment of Vrindaban. These are not like the escapist experience of some lovers of art. These are human experiences born out of her direct interface with different situations in life. If in *Ahiron, Nilkanhi Braja, Mamora Dhara Tarowal* and *Nangotha Shahar* she puts together the experiences picked up from the broad all-India canva, she paints an enchanting picture of the village life of Kamrup centering round the Satra in *Dantal Hatir Une Khowa Hawda*. In *Nilakanthi Braja,* she has penned a heart rendering narration of the sub-human condition."

— Editorial in *Aideur Jonaki Baat*, March, 1983.

❀ ❀ ❀ ❀ ❀

Creations beyond Assam border

"Mamoni Goswami is possibly the only modern Assamese prose-writer who has successfully picked up subject-matters for literary creations beyond the frontiers of Assam. Her wide outlook and strength of mind indicate a bold new step for our........... Some of Mamoni's expressions are indeed memorable. For example, 'the fragrance of her body is like that of the juice of freshly crushed sugarcane.' 'Could he devote that much of time to his wife as he did to his drinks?'

'The hands and feet of the two young daughers of the sweeper are as tender as the maize sapling and the bodies of the Khalasis are like those of wild buffaloes.'

'The Company's office building at the site has the look of a scare-crow in the cultivation field-red flags all around and slogans written with embers on the walls.'

The writer has given detailed account of certain events in a most detached manner and without any political bias. The subtle but frightening hint she gives towards the end by rubbing the rust off the sword is possibly necessary for the evolution of the theme. Yet it is hard to believe that the problems of the Harijans can be solved through murder and violence. Every renowned writer has a great responsibility towards the mother tongue. Mamoni Goswami has profusely used English and other non-Assamese words. It is hoped that she would be particular about using pure Assamese words."

— Review of *Ahiron* by Chandra Prasad Saikia in *Prakash*, January, 1983

❀ ❀ ❀ ❀ ❀

The pen and the sword

"The pen may or may not be mightier than the sword, but the two are not always opposed to each other. They can be in harmony even if the point of the pen is a little blunt and the sword a bit rusted as in the case of Dr. Indira Goswami. In her books, the functions of the writer's pen and the reformer's sword shade into each other. Dr. Goswami, who writes under the pseudo name Mamoni Raisom Goswami, got the Sahitya Akademi Award for 1982 for her Assamese novel *The Rusted Sword*.

The theme of *The Rusted Sword* is a long-drawn strike by the labourers of a construction company building an aqueduct over the river Sai in Rae Bareli. The strike fails. But the questions it throw up remain Mamoni's protest against the decaying social values. As Narayani, one of the characters in the novel, poignantly puts it, "Of what use are clean clothes when beneath them all is nakedness?"

— *Indian Express, Monday Diary*,
June 6, 1983

❀ ❀ ❀ ❀ ❀

A rare literary skill

"History of Assamese literature contains but only a few names of women writers. Fewer still are such among them as are powerful and fortnight. Mamoni Goswami has proved to be an exception. Emerging as a short story writer, Smt. Goswami has of late come to the limelight for a number of novels. In all these she has exhibited rare literary skill, courage and determination. Her novel *Mamare Dhara Tarowal* won her the Sahitya Akademi Award. The type of bold determination and authenticity with which the story is narrated and the characters developed is possibly unprecedented in Assamese literature.

In *Ardha Nogna Chorita*, Smt. Goswami presents a pen-picture of the inner life of a wealthy family with a same degree of authenticity, boldness and determination. The complex manner in which the theme has been developed as well as the internal conflict of the characters are evident all through the novel."

—Kamud Goswami.

A personal note on *Unfinished Autobiography*

"Her portrayal of Madhu Sequel is as tragic as her definition of squalor, misery and hypocrisy in Vrindaban — "The City of Gods". The portrayal is heart-breaking. But what has impressed me most is her character of a person. I congratulate her. There are not many good writers in the world with good character. The Assamese fraternity of creative writers can take pride in having her among them."

— Kartar Singh Duggal
Aprit 6, 1992

❀ ❀ ❀ ❀ ❀

Disarming autobiography

"Indira Goswami's book has all the makings of a magnificently disarming autobiography.. It stands out as a singularly frank, embarrasingly honest and sincere life story free from the usual celebratory, often self-justifying primeness. It is loudly surprising that her life story was read avidly by an admiring circle of readers when it first appeared in instalments in Assamese periodicals.

.... It is extraordinarily captivating, as well as disquieting, both fascinating and repelling in its native openness and uninhibitated nature...... The singularly honest and transparently sincere personality that Indira Goswami possesses — a novel — it touches and sounds one's heart. It can he said that such autobiographies are rarely written in Indian languages. It is really a wonderful and unique work. The translation is so good that it appears as if it was not a translated work, but an original one. Publication is also equally praiseworthy. The work will go a long way in the world of literature."

— Himanshu Joshi,
***Saptahik Hindustan,* March 29 to April 4, 1992**

Crossing river of fire

"After crossing the river of fire, Indira Goswami has successfully scaled so may hill tops. Her well-known novel *Mamare Dhara Tarowal* won the Sahitya Akademi Award. But in her autobiography, she has brought so many worlds together. She has won many laurels, including the Sahitya Akademi Award for literature.

'Writing is in my blood, in my veins. If I stop I will die of suffocation. Without my pen I will die...... Without my pen I will die...... With my writings I am free as a bird, to fly anywhere to be anyone, to understand anything.'

It is the river in which her emotions, pain and memory flow away from her, and become part of earth's eternal realities. In her loneliness the world has become as vital as a heartbeat."

— *The Times of India,* March 3, 1991

❀ ❀ ❀ ❀ ❀

Plumbing women minds

"But the question remains — can a male writer enter successfully into a woman's psyche? I tend to think that even the greatest men writers have failed to plumb the subliminal depth of a woman's mind and heart. This is evident from the work of Indira Goswami, who is now indisputably acknowledged as one of the most outstanding Assamese writers. And but for the commendable translation of her work into English by P. Kotoky and others, she would have remained unknown to non-Assamese readers. With a rare candour and courage, she lashes out, in her *Unfinished Autobiography*, against the entire fabric of male aggressiveness...... It is during her widowhood that she discovers that the measure of animality in men was much more than in women.

...... We watch her grow, in her early years, into womanhood. "I grew aware of my figure out day by day ..... At the age of twelve, my breasts has grown so much that I was terribly embarrassed when my father saw me taking a bath naked in my bathroom....." It is with the same fierce transparency that she says after losing her husband in an accident. "Who can ascertain the exact mind of a woman so suddenly hit by misfortune as I was? Who can determine how the abrupt end of a happy conjugal life affects the poor wife?......" It is during her widowhood that she discovers that the measure of animality in man, was much more than in women. It is this type of lecherous male that she encounters in Vrindavan, "The City of God", where man, in the barb of priest and saint, seeks only me flesh of women, especially the helpless young widows who frequent these places of worship in quest of spiritual solace. Helplessly, Indira cries out - "Indeed, it is not easy to understand, a man's cruel nature......"

...... *An Unfinished Authobiography* reads like a fictional narrative with its dramas, and suspense, its twist and turns, its portraiture of real men and women, who seem to be characters risen from the pages of a novel or a short story. A fascinating book to read, enjoy and preserve."

- Shiv K. Kumar,
***Hindustan Times*, May 25, 1991.**

❁ ❁ ❁ ❁ ❁

Ups and downs

"As you go through this autobiography it leaves a pleasant feeling in you. All the ups and downs of her life come alive here in a translucent and fearless way. The way she has put across things also attracts attention. She has her own style which sustains interrests.The language, too, is equally expressive and alturing. Readers should know the writers is the same Indira Goswami whose novel *Mamare Dhara Tarowal* won Sahitya Akademi Award in 1982.

In fact, this autobiography has the traits of a novel and that's why it sustains interest all through. It touches you in the raw, as it is also uplifting in effect. Autobiography writings is not an easy genre. It has its complexities. But Indira Goswami has turned it to her advantage by rising it to a higher pedestal from an individualistic account to an universal account. It brings out her struggles in most vivid details. It, in fact, does proud not only to the Assamese literature but to the entire Indian literature also."

— Jyotish Joshi, *Navabharat Times*, 1992

Extraordinary writing

"An extraordinary writing, Indira Goswami's *An Unfinished Autobiography* is extraordinarily captivating, as well as disquienting — both fascinating and repelling in its naive openness and uninhibited nature...... It is a honest transparently sincere personality that Indira Goswami possesses...... Reader will undoubtedly book forward to its sequel."

— *The Hindu*,
22 October, 1992

Solid social background

"Blessed with brains a writer's itch and a solid social background, Indira Goswami (Mamoni Raisom Goswami) came full circle to shine like a star in the literary and academic firmament of that great sub-continent of Bharathadesha.......

***Sunday Observer* in Sri Lanka**

Disintegration of power

"I fell that with the publication of the book *Datal Hatir Une Khowa Howda* (The Moth-eaten Howda of a Tusker) a great writer has emerged amidst us. Mamoni Goswami tells a wonderful story, a story of disintegration of power, of unbelievable suffering of men and women, and also of tremendous courage and the remendous pain that love brings. The characters so Assamese and yet so universal alive and kicking real and exciting, to say the least, kept me haunting for many days. It is an unforgettable work.

Prof. Sisir Kumar Das,
Tagore Professor, Delhi University

❀ ❀ ❀ ❀ ❀

Knots of opium-eaters

"It is not merely fortuitous that as soon as you turn the opening pages of this novel, you are face to face with an embience which is misty and does not allow you to look through. Yes, there is mist all around, as ther are dense forests with a variety of animals hollering in an awosome way. Then, there are uneven pathways lined with knots of opium-eaters, as there is a laper squatting near the bridge like an accured being. We also hear the wilings of the wrotched widows which come pouring out of the innards of their dilapidated houses. Besides, a myriad taboos of ritualism hold them in their vice-like grip.

There is the local of this novel which is inhabited by Indranath and some other characters. On occasions, we do find patches of moonlight here and there. as we also come across female beauty and experience ripples of unsullied joy rising in our heart, but for most of the time, we sufer the tradition society which needs to be ripped apart, and to an extent, a few characters do make an attempt in this direction. Ultimately, however, Giribala has tolay down her life, Indranath falls victim to his own men and Durga vanishes in the thin air because of her tuberculosis.

But this novel does not merely tell us the story of these characters. It has a vide spread a spans the entire society. Its reading is a unforgettable experience. Whenever my mind wanderc back to this sombre, penumbral and horrid atmosphere, I feel overpowered by awe.

Indira Goswami has turned out a powerful novel. She needs to be congratulated heartily. It will undoubtedly, be welcomed by the Hindi world."

Bhishma Sahni
New Delhi
August 12, 2000.

Cherished event

"Here, we are to honour some one who has always been a cherished event for us, the name of an author who has never ceased to fascinate us and haunt our imagination - we are talking about Dr. Indira Goswami or as we would be happy to call Mamoni baideu. This year's Jnanpith award to Dr. Indira Goswami is much-anticipated recognition of her achievement. Apart from being a scholar who is remarkable for her depth and intensity of intellect, it is the name of an author - nor a proper name, but an author's name that fascinates us.

What it is that fascinates us, if not a body of worlds and what that worlds evoke for us, transform us, the worlds that bear the name of an author we are talking about? It is the world of language that goes beyond language through language - it is the surplus world, the world of excess and transformation - the world of desires and horror, death and tendemess. But it is only through language that language evokes what language fails - a reality inaccessible to us but fascinates us as well. It is this abysmal secret of our inmost being - our limit experiences where word fails - that Indira Goswami's novels evoke in us whether in *Datal Hatir Uwe Khowa*

Haoda or *Eswari*. We are seemed to be pusshe to the limit in which we suddenly confront an abysmal world our in most being - that secret part in which things revel in pure nakedness - the indomitable lust, the horror at the inhumanity of the human world.

In *Datal Hatir Uwe Khowa Haoda* or elsewhere, it is this desire and horror that is evoked. It is a world in which things have worn out; the underlying structure to which an appeal can be made for social cohesion and integrity suddenly gives away to as if "the things fall apart/centre cannot hold". In this decadent world an appeal is made - not to the restoration of once established values which in the name of social cohesion does nothing but suppresses the very content of life, our desires and impuses - but an appeal is made to the very recreation of values, new values, transformation of values. In this inhuman world o fhumanity, every transgressive act that transgresses the given structure of norms and values is destroyed inhumanly - the result being the emptying out of the very content of life itself of which women are the most victims whether Damayanty or someone else. Slowly and gradually these women's lives were ruined and devastated; their simple human desires being condemned as transgressive. It is the horror of desire that constitutes the very fabric of a totalitarian society which is to be condemned - the world of father and the world the master.

But it is desire which horrifies the father and the master, it is this excess, this surplus that cannot be constrained in the law of father and the master which has the potentiality for every transformative act for every recreation of values, for every transformation of values. It is this excess, this surplus, this excessive human experience that is being evoked in Indira Goswami's novels. This trnsgression is evoked by means of a language that exceeds itself and pushes itself to the limit for the unnameable, for the solitude of the night where daylight fails. It is this communication in desire for an other that an ethical relationship is achieved. But even then, social custom stands as barrier. Thus in the short story *Offspring,* the unfullfilled woman hesitates to establishe and ethical relationship with an other even though the other is there only because of values given to us - values of purify in the name of caste.

Indira Goswami's novels are a ceaseless mumuring of such a a world in which exigency of recreation of values is revealed through evocationof people who suffer. It is this aspect of ethicality with tragic beauties that Indira Goswami's works will be of supreme importance to us.

- Satya Brata Das

❀ ❀ ❀ ❀ ❀

A charming personality

"I feel happy to welcome Dr. Indira Goswami, the recipient of the Jnanapitha Award and all the celebrities of Delhi who have gathered here for reception.

May I tell you that I have known Dr. Indira Goswami for a number of years and I have found her to be a unique person in many respects. She is a great writer in Assamia language and best-selers. Her scholarly works on many subjects and specially the research-oriented works on the *Ramayana* has fetched her great recognition all over the world. She has been invited to number of conferences within India and abroad on the subject of Ramayana. She has brought laurels to India by her works and presentation of the *Ramayana* in a wonderful manner.

Her own life has been one of hardwork pursuing research and teaching at the university and passing through the most difficult times in her life. Rising above the personal tragedies in her life, she shines like a brilliant star on the firmamant of Indian literature. Her autobiography is a testament to her great genius.

I feel happy to have the privilege to publish her books and having got cordial relations with a personality like her who is a great writer, a humanist and a charming personality.

With these words I offer this bouquet and shawl to her on behalf of the Federation and all of you."

D.N. Malhotra

(Text of the welcome speech given by Malhotra at the dinner arranged by the Federation of Indian publishers in honour of Dr. Indira Goswami)

❀ ❀ ❀ ❀ ❀

Not a Tantric

Devotees keep worshiping endlessly, those in meditation try to perceive the essence of our being beneath our bodies of flesh and blood. Countless priests have carefully prepared plates of delicious food offered to the dead. Those dead might have been heartless souls. But the loving heart which longed to find some solace remains unfullfilled after all this, worship and meditation. The father could not understand such worship or meditation to understand our being, he looked on somewhat puzzled. It didn't really interest him. He fondly watched his loving daughter, admiring her for all the fame she had won, for all that she had achieved.

A loving father listens carefully to the unconscious longings of his daughter. But he is not the one to dissect and analyses the mind of his daughter whom he loves so much. A father only bless and lovingly kisses the forehead of his daughter.

A father does not try to untangle, he is not caught in the intellectual web which tries to unequal things why not try also to listen to what the father may have to tell you ?

In his voice you will only hear his prayers to the Goddess of learning–Saraswati,

Saraswati–clad all in white,

You are not a creation of the gemes
    nor of flesh and blood
You are a creation of the poet's mind
    a pure child of the poetic imagination
Mamoni, you don't believe in the mother cult
    nor are you like a wild huntres.
You belong more the Buddhist tradition,
    So cease to care about name or fame
which is a part of the more mundane
    literary tradition which you should try
to leave behind you
    You had heard the sound of the chant
coming from the mountain cave
    "Mami Padam hoom"
the voice was deep as of thunder
    Sitting on adamantine 'Bajrasana,' deeply
meditating, someone had chanted that 'mantra.
    My dear daughter, the stone
shinning at the heart of the lotus
    flower is not a pearl.
It is a drop of tear which
    shines like a bright pearl
Mamoni, You are treading a simple path,
    which is the right path–it is the path of the Buddha.

With your own light try to get rid of the disgrace of animal sacrifice, get away from the tradition of blood and passion associated with the cult of the mother-worship.

The path of blood and passion is not the one of enlightenment. One day calling you away from a crowd.

I had said C Mamoni, you are like a swan swimming in the ocean of the 'Ramcharitmanas.'

The swan is the vehicle of Saraswati, Mamoni, go once to Dandakarayna and Chitrakut depicted so well in the Ramayana of Valmiki.

In the Dandakarayna forest, Lakshmana had built a cottage of leaves for Ram and Sita.

The 'Yagna' worship was done with deed meat after washing it clean of all blood stains. Then Ram and Sita entered that cottage of leaves.

Then in the beautiful forest of Chitrakut, Lakshmana had again made another cottage of leaves for Ram and Sita. This time no animal sacrifice was made at the time of entering the house. The religious ritual of entering the house was done by offering flowers to propitiate the Gods. Flowers were offered instead of the sacrifice of animals. In Dravidia language 'pu' means flower. The Sanskrit word 'pushp' is of Dravidian origin.

Dear Mamoni had opposed animal sacrifice in the Devi Temple in Kamrup.

Women : You are always an enigma, mother, wife, daughter are your three forms. Who has revealed the mystery of these three forms of the primordial woman,

Is it Buddha ? Kabir ? Rabindranath.... or may be on Mamoni?

Mamoni, surely you do know that I take you seriously and respect you for your work. You are a woman whose life's work is to build bridges of understanding so that people can forge ahead. And that is a great task and I admire you for it.

by Navkanta Barua

15

Face to Face

Dr Goswami and author exchanged views on different issues during an interview at her residence in 2001
Picture by Kamal Krishna

Q: What is your immediate reaction to the news that you bagged the prestigious Jnanpith Award? Do you think it is a proper recognition of your achievement?

Dr Goswami : I could not believe it when I got the news. Since my name was proposed for the Jnanpith Award several times earlier but was rejected in as many times. I never expected that I shall ever get the award. But I also got recognition from the people at large prior to getting this award, which I consider as my fortune. I am happy, everyone becomes happy on getting such an award. It will be a lie if I tell you that I am not happy.

Q: You are already known in different parts of the country as an eminent writer. Will the Jnanpith Award make a difference and enhance your reputation further?

Dr Goswami : Yes, it does so. The Jnanpith Award totally changes the scene. No other award in India is equivalent to it.

Q: Can it be considered a recognition for women-writers of the country?

Dr Goswami : I do not accept the division between man and woman. Don't mind, but I do not consider myself inferior to the male-writers.

Q: There has been a long gap between the award of the prize to Birendra Kumar Bhattacharya and the prize now conferred on you. Will it direct the attention of the country towards Assamese literature?

Dr Goswami : Definitely it will. I am not taking any pride, already a special issue of a magazine of Madhya Pradesh nemed *Punascha* is dedicated to me. After my winning the Jnanpith Award, the attention of the country will be directed more to the Assamese literature.

Q: What do you think is the vocation of the writer today? Does the writer has any responsibility to society?

Dr Goswami : Yes, the writer should bring into focus the ills of the society without any hesitation and fear. I have written against sacrifice without any fear. I have also penned stories and novels on militancy and bloodshed. I am planning to write more. But for that I shall have to delve into the psyche of the boys.

Q: People say you are rejecting Padmashri. Comment.

Dr Goswami : When I first heard the news about the Padmashri being awarded to me, I was surprised. Why now ? But I did not take the decision to refuse it right away. All awards are precious, all have their own dignity. However, after being conferred with the prestigious Jnanpith award last year, the Padmashri now appear quite incongruous to me.

As a writer, I hold the Jnanpith–one of the most prestigious literary awards of the country–in very high esteem.

The Padmashri would have been fine, had it come to me a year ago. Still, I was hesitant. Will it be right if I refuse the award ? Will my action make me appear too vain ?

But it did not take very long for my doubts so disappear. Everybody I met–my well-wishers and fans–was unanimous : "The Padmashri is not for me. Not now".

Wherever I have been in the past few days–to moffusil towns, interio- or villages and Guwahati–the reaction of the people has been the same. I could sense the feeling of disappointment among them. The ultimate decision, I must say, was not only mine but also of the people.

After I made up my mind, very modestly, I told the people who took the decision to honour me that I cannot accept the Padmashri. But I did not forget to thank them. I tried to be as polite as I could. Those were difficult words to say, but I had no other option. It is a matter of self respect of my fans and well-wishers. Any award or honour to me, ultimately belongs to them. For, they have made me what I am today.

The other day, a delegation arrived from a village near Tihu.They were organising a function where they planned to felicitate me. I was slightly unwell, so I turned down their request.

The disappointment in their faces was simply unbelievable. One of the ladies in the delegation started crying out aloud. They had come with such high hopes, everything was dashed by a single sentence of mine. How could I say no to people who love me so much ?

I went that day and I am now happy that I did. It was a wonderful trip, though extremely tiring.

Such was the condition of the road to the village that, at times, I felt as if the vehicle would overturn. And I was thinking : these people travelled more than 100 km just to have me in their midst. It would have been very ungrateful of me not to have come.

Such love and affection keep me going, give inspiration for my writing. These people are the protagonists of my write-ups, their homes the backdrop. And I believe that it is my duty to ensure that the people of my State walk with their heads high.

I took a very conscious decision in rejecting the Padmashri.

And I have no regrets.

Appendix

Unpublished Letter

(1)

To, August 22, 2001

Smt. Indira Goswami,
D19, 29/31, Provyn Road
Delhi University Staff Quarters
Delhi - 110 007

Dear Mamoni,

Please accept out love, affection and hearty congratulations for your excellent accievements. I am almost bed-rideen for over a month. I heard it from my wife who has collected all the clippings published in all the newspapers. We have preserved them.

My wife desires to convey her feelings to you :

A dream is a daring adventure, a journey to carry you for. For when you can hold a dream in your heart, you surely can reach any star !

"A dream is a beautiful vision. That looks beyond what you can see. Then lifts you and guides you and grows strong inside you to help you to be all you can be.

A dream is your door to tomorrow. A secret reflection of you. A threshold that leads to a wonderful future where nothing too good to be true....."

Justice K. Lahiri
(Mrs. Krishna Lahiri)
Retd Chief Justice, Gauhati High Court

(2)

To,
Professor Indira Goswami,
Department of Modern Indian Language
University of Delhi,
Delhi - 110 007.

From:
University of Delhi
Deepak Nayyar
Vice-Chancellor
No.VC/2001/303
31st July 2001

Dear Professor Goswami,

I was delighted to read the wonderful news that you have received the Jnanpith Award. It is a tribute to your rich literary talents. It is also a great honour for the University of Delhi. The news is a source of joy and pride for all of us in the university community. And I am sure that it would inspire successive generations of schclars to follow in your footsteps. On behalf of the University of Delhi, I would like to contratulate you for this richly deserved honour.

With best wishes.

Yours sincerely,
Deepak Nayyar

Poem dedicated to Mamoni Raison Goswami

All the hours of the night,
Like a drunk I roamed,
With the earth for company, in faltering steps,
In search of you.

The wind, too, wanted to join me.
In what distant rampart
Are you clining your head in sleep,
O thou, lady of serious love ?
The wind, too, wanted to join me;
In what distant rampart
Are you reclining your head steep,
Thou lady of serious love ?

Nilam Kumar